Enneagram Made Easy

A Spiritual Journey of Self-Discovery to Uncover Your True Personality Type and Become the Healthy Version of Yourself

Michael Wilkinson

Disclaimer

This book is not aimed at offering any medical advice or representing medical treatment or advice from your personal healthcare provider. Readers should consult their personal physicians or licensed health professionals concerning their medical conditions and treatments. The author shall not be held responsible or liable for any misuse or misinterpretation of the information provided in this book. The information is not intended for diagnosis, cure or treatment of any ailment.

Be reminded that the author of this book is not a medical professional/doctor/therapist. Only opinions on the basis of personal experiences and research are referenced. The author does not provide any medical advice or prescription of any treatments. Consult your doctor for any medical or health issues.

It is important to note that I research all of the material in my books to bring you the highest quality material. Unfortunately, there are substandard, cheap outsourced books on the non-fiction market nowadays which are developed by different Internet marketing organizations. My aim is to ensure you are provided with only high quality contents as **I do not compromise the high quality of my books**.

Table of Contents

Also, if you haven't downloaded your free book already:

The Growth Mindset: How To Become The Best Version of Yourself

To help speed up your personal transformation, I have prepared a special gift for you!

Download my full 88-page e-book "The Growth Mindset: How To Become The Best Version of Yourself"

Visit this Link:

https://www.developsuccessmindset.com/mindset-gift/

Introduction

We are excited to take you to this journey of self-discovery to find out which personality type you are and find out new things you never knew about yourself!

Have you been struggling to find your place in this world? Do you question what makes you feel so different from the people around you? Or have you been trying to relate to someone special but just can't seem to find a way to make things "click" with that person?

The answers to these dilemmas and countless others lie in this guide to the Enneagram!

At this point, you might be saying "Any-a-what??!" Or maybe you have already heard of it but you're not sure what it has to do with you. If you are unsure, please be reassured that you have come to the right place! No matter what you're hoping to learn about yourself or other people, help is here.

At first glance, the Enneagram is a symbol. But it's so much more than that! It's a tool for personal transformation and strengthening the ties that bind us together. Millions have witnessed its power to transform lives! People see their own experiences reflected clearly in it and they have had their eyes opened to truths that were right in front of them all along.

The following chapters will discuss everything you need to know about the Enneagram and how to become the best possible version of yourself. You'll learn how to identify your own basic personality type. And you'll learn how to use that information to grow personally, improve relationships and your work life, and relate to others on a profound level.

The nine personality types are: Reformer, Peacemaker, Challenger, Helper, Achiever, Individualist, Investigator, Loyalist, and Enthusiast. Perhaps you can already guess what your type might be by name alone. Prepare to be completely blown away when you learn your true type and what it means.

There are plenty of books on this subject on the market, so thanks again for choosing this one! Every effort was made to ensure it is full of as much useful information as possible. Please enjoy!

Part 1: Getting Our Feet Wet, Enneagram Style

Chapter 1: The Enneagram – What Is It and How Do We Use It?

A Brief History of the Enneagram
To understand the Enneagram, it might help you to know a bit about where it came from. The word Enneagram comes from the Greek words *ennea*, which means "nine," and *gramma*, meaning "model," "points," or something "written" or "drawn."

The early origins of Enneagram are greatly disputed and not officially known. Some claim that the symbol originated in the ancient mathematics of the Pythagoreans, some 4000 years ago. Others believe that the philosopher Philo introduced a version of the Enneagram to esoteric Judaism, where it later became a part of the Tree of Life in the Kabbalah discipline. Still, others believe it originated in Islamic Sufi mysticism. It also seems to include aspects of ancient mystical Christianity, Taoism, Buddhism, and Greek philosophy.

The Enneagram's modern form and use are credited to a few specific sources. George Gurdjieff, a Greek-Armenian spiritual teacher, used the Enneagram symbol to explain the laws of creation and aspects of the universe. He probably first saw the symbol when he visited a monastery in Afghanistan during the 1920s.

The current system of Enneagram personality typing started with Oscar Ichazo, who founded a school of self-realization in Chile in the 1950s and 60s. He developed the basic principles of Enneagram theory from ideas of early Christianity, mystical Judaism, and classic Greek philosophies. A student of Ichazo in 1970 was psychiatrist Claudio Naranjo, who brought the

Enneagram to the U.S. Its popularity spread throughout North America within a few years.

In 1973, an American teacher named Don Riso added insights from modern psychology to Enneagram teachings. In 1988, Russ Hudson joined him and they developed the personality typing system of today. After continually experiencing its power as a tool for understanding ourselves and those around us, Riso and Hudson formed The Enneagram Institute in 1997 to further research and development. Currently, the institute develops and sponsors workshops and training so the power of the Enneagram can keep improving human lives.

An observation that modern psychological research has made about the Enneagram is its incredible accuracy in terms of insights into human nature. Not only does it confirm what has already been discovered about the psyche, but it can also anticipate the knowledge found in modern psychological diagnostic tools.

In short, the Enneagram has ancient and mysterious origins, but its modern personality typing is very impressive!

The Enneagram's Shape

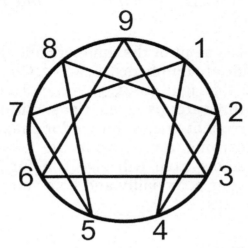

Without the elegantly simple geometric shape of the Enneagram, we would not have a thorough understanding of the nine basic personality types and how they interconnect and relate to each other. So let's take a look at it for a moment.

On the outside is a circle with nine points spread equally around the circle. It's important that all nine personality types are connected in the circle because a human being has the potential for any of these personalities.

On each side of a type lies another potential type, and these are called *wings*. For example, the wings of type 7 are the numbers 6 and 8. Although you may be a type 7, you may lean heavily towards either 6 or 8 – this leaning is called your wing. You'll learn about this in Chapter 2.

Inside the circle is an equilateral triangle (all three sides of equal length), which connects the points 3, 6, and 9. The second shape inside the circle is an irregular hexagonal figure (six-sided figure with unequal sides) that connects the rest of the points in this order: 1-4-2-8-

5-7-1. This order will become important in Chapter 2 when we discuss *directions of integration and disintegration.*

Notice the placement of the numbers one through nine. On the left side are numbers 5, 6, and 7. On the top are 8, 9, and 1. On the right are 2, 3, and 4. The 9 types are divided into three groups called triads. Within each triad, the three personality types have a dominant emotion in common. Learning more about the triad that your personality stems from will give you further valuable insight into your personality and help you on your path to self-awareness.

What Sets The Enneagram Apart?

You've probably seen a lot of personality tests. But the Enneagram is not just a test. It's a conceptualization of the human experience. It explains how all types are connected. It tells *why* we think, act, and feel certain ways instead of just *how* we think, act, and feel.

All those personality tests may tell you what you are likely to do in certain situations or how you may feel when faced with certain situations. But wouldn't it be nice to understand the *why* behind those thoughts and actions?

The Enneagram teachings are the first of any personality typing systems to reveal the basic primal instincts, fears, and survival mechanisms that drive us to become who we are. It's a tool for not only understanding your personality but for unlocking the potential for growth within yourself. By understanding how you became who you are and what drives you, you can conquer fears holding you back and cope with negative emotions that you previously tried to avoid.

The Enneagram is important as a spiritual tool. Whether you have a strong faith in one God or believe in the broader, innate spirituality of the universe, you can use what you learn to find spiritual enlightenment. Unlike many psychological tools, the teachings of the Enneagram address character defects. It helps us understand how we can be held captive to our fears and basic passions. It aids us in finding ways to rise above our character defects. Consequently, you learn where you need spiritual healing and discover how to reach this healing.

Enneagram is also an important tool for interacting with other people in your life! Whether you want to understand your business associates, enhance your romantic relationship, or improve your parenting style, you can find the answers here. By gaining insights into the motivations of others, you can learn how to interact with them harmoniously. So keep reading!

How to Read this Book

You do not have to read this entire book word-for-word if you don't want to. It may be helpful and interesting for some people to read the whole thing. But you may prefer to just read about your own type and the types of a few key people in your life. It's up to you!

However, we do recommend that you stick with us for another couple of chapters first. In Chapter 2, you'll learn what it means to have a basic personality type and how to get the most out of learning about your specific type. Then, in Chapter 3, you'll get to determine your most likely personality type out of the 9.

Chapters 4 through 12 each cover a specific personality type, so here's where you can jump around as much as you please. You can just go to your specific type, or maybe, you'll want to read about your possible wings as well. At the end of each chapter, you'll get relationship hints for each type.

Chapter 2: The Basic Personality Type

The Nine Types

You'll read in-depth descriptions of each personality types in later chapters, but here are some very brief descriptions. Some authors call these personalities by alternate names. Here, they are listed by the Riso-Hudson type names (so named after the two founders of The Enneagram Institute):

- **Type 1:** The Reformer – self-controlled, rational, principled, and perfectionist.

- **Type 2:** The Helper – caring, generous, genuine, people-pleasing, and possessive.

- **Type 3:** The Achiever – competitive, success-oriented, appearance-driven, and focused.

- **Type 4:** The Individualist – sensitive, expressive, creative, unique, dramatic, temperamental, and romantic.

- **Type 5:** The Investigator – innovative, curious, perceptive, quiet, withdrawn, and careful.

- **Type 6:** The Loyalist – responsible, anxious, committed, trustworthy, and suspicious.

- **Type 7:** The Enthusiast – versatile, optimistic, social, adventurous, impulsive, and distractible.

- **Type 8:** The Challenger – decisive, confident, dominating, independent, intense, and confrontational.

- **Type 9:** The Peacemaker – reassuring, accommodating, easygoing, supportive, complacent, and avoids conflicts.

Inside you lay the potential for all these personality types. That is why you may be able to relate to many or even all of them. However, as you take the test and keep reading, one of them should seem closest to your true nature. This one type is your *basic personality type*.

Which type becomes your dominant personality is influenced by several things. Before you are born, genetics affect the ways you are likely to think, feel, and act. Although environmental factors that influence you after birth are important, most experts agree that your dominant type was determined before you were born.

After birth, your basic personality type continued to be shaped by outside influences. Your environment and the way that you were raised played a huge part in shaping your *defense mechanisms*, which are important parts of your personality type. Everyone learns to behave and react to their environment differently, and we all leave childhood with a unique view of the world.

Before going further, there are a couple of important things to understand. Even though the types are represented by numbers, no personality is more important or better than any other personality. It's okay if you don't relate to every part of the description of your dominant personality type. We all fluctuate regularly in spiritual and emotional health, and you will relate more to some traits than others at various times in your life. *However*, no one ever changes from one principal type of personality to another. Not ever.

The Triads

As you read in the previous chapter, the nine personalities are divided into three sets of three groups called triads. The chapters about the personalities are grouped by these triads. The triads are called the *Instinctive* Triad, the *Feeling* Triad, and the *Thinking* Triad. Within each triad, the three basic personality types have specific underlying emotions in common.

This book is organized so that the three Triads are grouped together, so the order of the nine personalities is as follows: 8, 9, 1, 2, 3, 4, 5, 6, and 7.

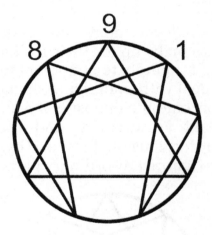

The Instinctive Triad – Types 8, 9, and 1

For the three personalities, anger is the dominant emotion in the Instinctive Triad. Each of the personalities deals with their anger differently. When an Eight feels anger, they tend to act on it almost immediately in a physical way, such as yelling or acting aggressively. In contrast, a Nine denies their anger and focuses on the other people in their lives. Ones try to control their anger and often turn it inwards upon themselves.

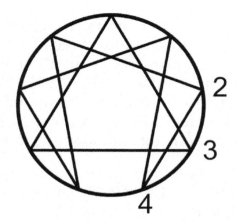

The Feeling Triad – Types 2, 3, and 4

In the Feeling Triad, your dominant emotion is *shame*. A type Two tries to make up for their feelings of shame by people-pleasing (attempts to get others to like and want them). Threes deal with underlying shame by denying it and trying to become the opposite of a shameful person through constant achievement and success. A Four avoids shame by focusing on theirs and by creating a kind of fantasy life to ignore any ordinary parts of their life.

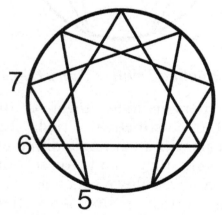

The Thinking Triad – Types 5, 6, and 7

The third triad deals with *anxiety*. Type Five suffers from anxiety about dealing with the outside world, and they cope by withdrawing from the world. A Six can be highly anxious, especially when it comes to trusting their own minds and instincts. They can succumb to this anxiety at times, but some Sixes may suddenly confront their fear and defy it. Sevens have fears about their inner negative emotions, like pain and loss. They deal with it by avoiding negative emotions and seeking stimulating activity and many distractions.

Traps, Avoidances, Idealizations, and Core Beliefs

In the description of each basic personality type, you'll read about *traps, avoidances, and idealizations*. To avoid confusion later, we'll define and explain these terms now.

Each personality type of the Enneagram has a *trap* – some focus or obsession that keeps you from making personal progress and growing spiritually. For example, a type One can be so obsessed with perfection and making things right that they are not able to see beyond their own self-imposed standards.

Avoidances are feelings and ideas that members of each personality type do their very best to avoid at all costs. Essentially, avoidances are our deep fears. A type Three will go to great lengths to avoid feeling like a failure while the behavior of type Seven is centered around avoiding any kind of emotional pain. These avoidances are closely linked to the traps defined in the paragraph above. Our avoidances are things that we need to experience growth.

Idealizations are the images that each personality type tries to present to the world, the standard that their behavior is focused on living up to, or what they believe

15

to be the most important trait a person can exhibit. For example, an Eight does their best to project an image of strength, so their idealization is "I am a strong person."

Your traps, avoidances, and idealizations exist because of your basic personality type's *core belief* system. Your core belief is your perspective of the world, the filter through which you experience life and prioritize what you believe are the most desirable traits and behaviors. Our core beliefs are usually unconscious, so we are not aware of their influence on our personalities.

Wrapping your head around all of these traits of the different personality types can take a little practice, but it will begin to make more sense as you read about your own type and realize how accurately your experiences are described in your type's chapter.

Vices/Passions

Each type's unique characteristics lead them to have unique weaknesses, which many experts list under the labels of *vices or passions*. These are the tendencies that can hinder our spiritual growth and lead us astray from the more noble characteristics of our types. An example of this can be seen in Eights, who sometimes, have the passion of lust. This isn't necessarily sexual lust; rather, it is a term for *intensity*. Eights crave the feeling of being fully alive. They tend to fully engage and exert their influence in everything they do. However, this intensity can be too aggressive and overwhelming.

Wings

Earlier, we mentioned *wings*, which are the numbers on either side of each personality type. While you may have one dominant personality type, no one's traits ever fall entirely into one category. Most people find that they are a mix of their dominant personality type plus one of the two types on either side. If you are a Five, you may find that you also identify with many characteristics of either Four or Six.

Your wing type adds important elements to your overall personality. Sometimes, these wing traits complement those of your dominant type, and sometimes, they are even in opposition to each other. It is very important to study the wing type so that you can truly gain a better understanding of yourself or another person that you are learning about.

Levels of Development

Another factor of personality types that make each individual unique is the *levels of development* within each type. This may seem complicated and confusing at first glance, but it's important to discuss because your personality's levels of development are critical to the personal growth you desire!

In each type is nine levels of development (don't confuse this with the nine dominant types!). Just like the triads, these levels come in three sets of three. The healthy range, average range, and the unhealthy range all have three development levels:

	Level 1	The Level of Liberation
Healthy	Level 2	The Level of Psychological Capacity
	Level 3	The Level of Social Value
	Level 4	The Level of Imbalance/ Social Role
Average	Level 5	The Level of Interpersonal Control
	Level 6	The Level of Overcompensation
	Level 7	The Level of Violation
Unhealthy	Level 8	The Level of Obsession and Compulsion
	Level 9	The Level of Pathological Destructiveness

You'll learn more about the levels of each type in the specific chapters.

By learning about your personality type, you will make a start at becoming healthier. Recognizing how your personality shapes your worldview is a first step in becoming more and aware of yourself, your thoughts, and your environment. Countless people have learned that the more they learn about their dominant type, the more they can free themselves of damaging emotions and beliefs and see themselves accurately.

Just imagine what your own personal growth experience might be once you have learned about your type and begin to make progress!

Directions of Disintegration (Stress) and Integration (Growth)

As we noted in the description of the Enneagram's structure, the nine points are not connected at random but in a very specific pattern. The order of connection represents how each type of person tends to behave under different circumstances.

The points on the equilateral triangle are 3, 6, and 9. In a clockwise direction, the sequence is 9-3-6-9. This is the direction of integration, and it shows how individuals behave in times of healthy personal growth. For example, a healthy Three under secure conditions will display some of the characteristics of a Six.

In the opposite direction, the order of the triangle is 9-6-3-9, and this is the direction of disintegration or stress. It shows how a person will behave in particularly stressful situations. For example, an average Nine under long-term stress will behave more like an average Six, and an unhealthy Three under stressful conditions will begin to act like an unhealthy Nine.

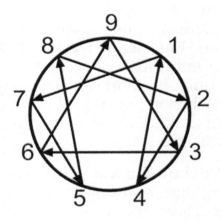

Integration Arrows

The remaining six points form an irregular hexagon with overlapping lines that cannot be followed in a clockwise or counter-clockwise direction. However, they do have a

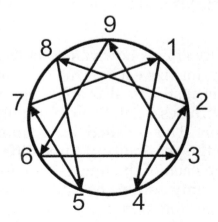

specific Direction of Integration (Growth): 1-7-5-8-2-4-1. And they have a Direction of Disintegration (Stress): 1-4-2-8-5-7-1. As with the triangle, these directions show how people of each type behave during times of personal growth or under conditions of long-term stress.

Disintegration Arrows

These Directions of Integration and Disintegration are not just theoretical! They have been observed by psychologists and Enneagram teachers time and again as they work with individuals of each of the nine different types. As you think back on your own experiences, you may be able to better understand your past behaviors under stressful conditions or during times of healthy personal growth.

Instinctual Variants, a.k.a. "Subtypes"
One more thing that makes us each unique is our *three basic instincts*. These are in each human being and are almost as necessary to life as breathing oxygen. These are the *social instinct* (for forming bonds with other people and social structure in a community), the *sexual instinct* (for forming one-to-one bonds and reproducing), and the *self-preservation instinct* (this is the instinct we use especially for needs and threats to preserve our own life and body.)

Your personality affects how you react to these instincts and how you prioritize each of the three needs. In turn, the three basic instincts also affect the way that your personality expresses itself. Each of us tends to prioritize only one instinct. This is called our *dominant instinct or subtype*. With the possibility of three different dominant instincts within each of the nine personality types, there are really twenty-seven possible combinations of personality type and dominant instinct. Add to those twenty-seven combinations are the possible wing types and levels of development, and there are a lot of unique personalities!

If you think about all you've learned so far, you'll see that the Enneagram shows how fluid and connected all the personalities really are. Your behavior can change based on whether you are in stressful conditions or conditions that encourage spiritual growth. Your psychological health can change, causing you to move up or down the levels of development within your personality type. And your wing personality type can express itself at times while remaining hidden at others. If you had any concerns about whether Enneagram's personality typing would label you or "put you in a box," hopefully, you can now see that the opposite is true. With the help of the Enneagram, you can unlock knowledge about the complexity and fluidity of your personality and discover secrets to your mind's inner workings – and the inner workings of the important people in your life!

Chapter 3: What's Your Number? The Type Quiz

This is a short quiz to help you determine your basic personality type. There are longer, more in-depth tests available, for a fee, from various sources online and in print. After scoring your quiz, we recommend that recommended that you read the chapters about your top three types in the next part of this book.

Instructions for the Quiz:
Get a spare piece of paper and write out numbers 1 through 36. For each number (starting on the next page), write the letter next to the statement that is most true for you. If a statement such as " It has often been easy for other people to upset me," for example, seems to describe you better than "It has typically taken quite a lot for other people to upset me," write down the letter of that statement.

Keep in mind that for each number, both statements may have described you at one point or another in isolated incidents. However, think about which statement describes you more accurately in general and most often in the past.

When taking this type of quiz, it has often helped people to think of how they behaved in their early 20s. Remember that this quiz is about your gut reactions and behavior, not occasional feelings or times that you have been influenced by others.

Remember that there are no "right" answers and no personality type is better than any other. Each one has its own virtues and temptations. Also, this test doesn't determine whether you are psychologically healthy or unhealthy. Just answer the questions honestly and quickly, without over-analyzing the meaning behind the answers. Be as spontaneous as you can in answering.

Someone who knows you very well can also help you discover your personality in case there is a tie in your scores. It usually takes ten minutes or less to finish the quiz. Instructions for scoring and determining your type are at the end of the quiz.

Also, remember that this fun and short personality quiz is not scientifically based. Many factors can influence your results, so they are not guaranteed.

The Enneagram Type Indicator Quiz

*For each question, below, choose **ONE** of the two statements. Record the letters representing your answers on a spare sheet of paper. (for example, for number 1, record letter "A" if the first statement describes you better and "F" if the second statement describes you more closely)*

1. G. I am afraid of getting too involved with people, because it may lead to conflict or confrontation.
   B. I am afraid of not being involved enough with people, because I want them to depend on me heavily.

2. F. I have great knowledge of some subjects, which has been helpful to others at times.
   E. I have great strength and can make decisions in a crisis, which has been helpful to others at times.

3. F. For the most part, I am usually intensely focused on the task at hand   and unwilling to change my plans.
   H. For the most part, I am usually looking for the next fun thing and willing to change my plans at a moments' notice.

4. C. It has often been easy for other people to upset me.
   G. It has typically taken quite a lot for anyone to upset me.

5. E. I like to take charge of situations and provide the strength that others need.
   D. I like to do the best I possibly can in every situation, and often my best feels like it isn't good enough.

6. E. I have learned to be strong by surviving many challenges that life has thrown at me.
   D. I have high ideals of proper behavior for myself and others, and I am disappointed when these ideals are not met.

7. B. I enjoy being emotionally and physically intimate with people, openly showing affection when possible.
   F. I enjoy keeping my distance from people, and I do not blend well with others.

8. B. I tend to focus more on fostering friendships than accomplishments.
   I. I tend to focus more on fostering accomplishments than friendships.

9. I. I have been opportunistic, only welcoming new experiences if they will benefit me.

H. I have been a fun-seeker, only welcoming new experiences if they seem exciting.

10. A. I have typically been too self-centered, often not noticing other people.
    G. I have typically moved the focus away from me and onto others too much.

11. A. I have usually had a good imagination and have often over-dramatized situations in my head.
    C. I have usually viewed situations from a practical and realistic point of view.

12. C. I have tended to lack confidence in myself.
    D. I have tended to be over-confident in myself.

13. I. I have typically been able to compartmentalize my feelings and focus on the task at hand.
    A. If I have strong feelings, I have typically needed to sort through these emotions before I can focus on anything else.

14. A. I have felt misunderstood and alone, unwilling to speak my mind.
    H. I have been typically brave enough to say things that others wish they could.

15. I. I am usually able to further my ambitions by attracting people with my charm and diplomacy.
    D. I am usually unable to be particularly charming; because of my high moralistic ideals, I prefer a more formal and direct approach to people.

16. F. I have had a very difficult time being decisive.

D. I have been very decisive, and have had a difficult time allowing for any flexibility in my ideas.

17. B. I love to welcome new friends into my life with open arms and hospitality.
A. I have trouble mixing with others, and I keep my personal thoughts to myself.

18. C. I think through things carefully and approach tasks one step at a time.
H. I tend to "leap before I look," preferring adventure to caution.

19. B. I truly enjoy being around others and lending a helping hand.
D. I take a fairly serious approach to life and prefer to discuss the morality of issues.

20. F. I am most interested in being independent and seeking facts.
G. I am most interested in keeping peace and stability in my environment.

21. E. I have often been quick to confront others.
G. I have often avoided confrontations at all costs.

22. H. When I make a commitment, I fear that I am missing out on something better.
E. When I get close to someone, I fear letting down my guard.

23. C. I tend to be very hesitant to make commitments.
E. I tend to be very bold, to the point of over-powering those around me.

24. A. I tend to keep myself apart from others.

E. I tend to be somewhat bossy.

25.G. If something in my world is not at peace, I tend to numb myself to the problem with some comforting activity.
H. If something in my world is not at peace, I tend to indulge myself in some sort of treat.

26. C. I like to choose friends that I can trust implicitly, and they can expect the same from me.
I. I do not like to depend on people; I prefer to be self-sufficient.

27.F. I have tended to be distracted and absent-minded.
A. I have tended to be dramatic and emotional.

28. E. I enjoy a healthy debate among friends.
B. I enjoy being a source of comfort and support for friends.

29. H. I am usually extroverted and eager to enjoy activities with others.
D. I am usually very disciplined and strive to follow the rules.

30. A. I do not like drawing attention to myself.
I. I like showing off and getting attention for my talents.

31.F. I am more interested in acquiring knowledge than worldly materials.
C. I am more interested in being sure of my security than in pursuing any hobbies or passions.

32.A. In disagreements with others, I like to escape into my own private thoughts and fantasies.

E. In disagreements with others, I like to be confrontational.

33. G. I tend to be a "pushover" to keep the peace.
D. I tend to have high expectations of others, and I do not compromise these expectations easily.

34. H. I have a quick wit and optimistic attitude.
B. I am a truly supportive and generous friend.

35. I. I am great at impressing people I have just met.
F. I am great at displaying my knowledge in my chosen field of interest.

36. C. I have been known as a skeptic, rarely or never swayed by emotions.
B. I have been known to be sentimental and easily swayed by emotions.

Scoring Your Quiz:

Add the number of each of the letters (A through I) you have on your piece of paper. If you have taken the quiz correctly and chosen one statement for each question, 36 should be the total of all of the numbers added together. If this is not your total, check your answers or your arithmetic again.

Each type of personality is represented by letters as shown below. Take note that *they are not in numerical order and are randomized*:

A = Type 4 (The Individualist)

B = Type 2 (The Helper)

C = Type 6 (The Loyalist)

D = Type 1 (The Reformer)

E = Type 8 (The Challenger)

F = Type 5 (The Investigator)

G = Type 9 (The Peacemakor)

H = Type 7 (The Enthusiast)

I = Type 3 (The Achiever)

The goal of the quiz is to discover your basic personality type out of the nine types. Answering the questions accurately and honestly will give you your type based on the top three scores. The following chapters include the description of each type. Check them out so that you can confirm your results.

Further resources will be given at the end of this book so that you can continue your research!

You can still review and double-check your answers if you got unclear results, or read about the different types so you can decide which ones most closely resembles your personality.

Part 2: Diving In –
Learning About the Types

Please note that this book is organized so that the three Triads are grouped together, so the order of the nine personalities is as follows: 8, 9, 1, 2, 3, 4, 5, 6, and 7. For a review of what the personalities in each Triad have in common, please refer back to Chapter 2.

The Instinctive Triad
(Types 8, 9 & 1)

Chapter 4: Type 8 – The Challenger

Type 8 Checklist: *How many of the following statements are true for you?*

- You are confident in yourself and assertive.
- You "shoot from the hip" when you speak.
- You are often the first to take charge of a situation.
- You are resourceful and decisive.
- You have protective instincts.
- You have a big heart and like to "take people under your wing."
- You feel you must control your environment, including the people around you.
- You can become self-centered and dominate or intimidate people.
- You sometimes have trouble controlling your temper.
- You fear to be vulnerable or controlled.
- You can inspire people and improve their lives with your strength.
- You want a lot out of life and feel prepared to go out and get it.
- You want to be financially independent and can have trouble working for someone else.
- You have a hard time trusting anyone right away.

- You have a strong sense of right and wrong and a strong desire for truth and justice.

If you can relate to more than half of the above statements, chances are that you are an Eight or you have a strong Eight wing. Keep reading to learn more about your type!

Core Belief

The belief that drives your behavior is that the world is an unjust place in which weak or innocent people are taken advantage of. Only the strong survive!

Avoidance: *Weakness*

You avoid weakness and being vulnerable. This avoidance highlights your basic fear of being controlled by others; you feel that if you expose any vulnerability, others might use that vulnerability to control you in some way.

Trap: *Enforcing Justice*

You can become so preoccupied with enforcing justice and/or protecting those around you that you are not focused on where you need to develop personally and spiritually.

Idealization: *I am strong.*

This is the image that you wish to project to the world. Doing so helps you avoid the thing you fear, appearing vulnerable.

Defense Mechanism: *Denial*

Denial is the refusal to accept certain realities, thoughts, or feelings. You use denial to protect the sensitivity and vulnerability underneath your tough outer surface of strength and control. If you feel a hint of weakness or powerlessness, you kill those emotions with the powerful defense mechanism of denial.

Passion: *Lust* (Intensity)

As a person who values physical strength, you want to feel intensely alive. You want to be fully engaged in life, and you don't appreciate people who only go through the motions. This can be good, but your intensity can become aggression, which overwhelms and intimidates others.

Description

You enjoy taking on challenges, and you like to challenge others through encouragement for them to improve their abilities. Sometimes, you also challenge authority. You have strong protective instincts for the people who are close to you. You stand up for what is right and speak your mind when you feel that justice is not being served.

As a member of the *Instinctive Triad*, your emotional issues center on anger, which you act on quickly in a physical way, such as speaking forcefully, yelling, or acting aggressively. Even if you are not violent or physically harmful, your forceful expressions of anger can be frightening to some people.

You are a natural leader. You excel at taking charge and getting things done. Many people find you to be a good leader because your strong sense of justice leads you to treat everyone fairly. However, at times, you can become domineering and intimidating.

You have strong willpower and seemingly unlimited energy, which contribute to your natural charisma. You also use these qualities to keep people from hurting you. From childhood, you learned to keep people at arm's length and display strength. You feel that being in charge and being strong will protect you from emotional pain.

Wings

The personalities to either side of you on the Enneagram are Seven, the Enthusiast, and Nine, the Peacemaker. An Eight with a stronger Seven-Wing has been labeled "The Maverick" by some, and Eight with a stronger Nine-Wing has been labeled "The Bear." Read the chapters on these personalities to decide if you identify more strongly with one of these wings.

Directions of Integration and Disintegration

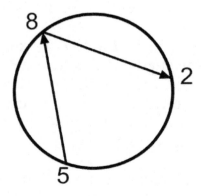

Your direction of integration is towards type Two, the Helper. This means that when you are emotionally healthy, you exhibit qualities of a healthy Two. When you recognize that your tough outer shell isolates you from others and begin opening yourself up to a few, others discover your generosity and warmth. You want to express your love and support for the people in your world.

If you are less emotionally healthy but in secure conditions, you may display the traits of an average Two. You can show your emotional side to a few people who are very close to you while still appearing strong and impervious in public. You may also become somewhat manipulative (like an average or unhealthy Two) as you try to hold on to the people who are close to you.

Your direction of disintegration is towards type Five, the Investigator. Your first reaction to stress as an Eight is to tackle the immediate challenge. However, you may eventually become overwhelmed by the effort. If you become too stressed, you might retreat from your usual aggressive approach and isolate yourself. This can help you to assess the problem, but if it lasts for too long or the stress is too great you may become colder and more cynical, like unhealthy Fives.

Levels of Development

The following is a very brief breakdown of your levels of development as an Eight, so you can begin to recognize your psychological health and warning signs of emotional deterioration.

- **Healthy**
  - **Level 1 (at your best):** You restrain yourself well and show mercy. You submit to leadership. You are a loyal friend and you sacrifice yourself for loved ones. You are emotionally open. You do not need to constantly assert yourself or control anyone. You have heroic qualities.
  - **Level 2:** You are resourceful and self-starting, with a passion that keeps you going. You stand up for what you need. You are confident and assertive, not intimidating.
  - **Level 3:** Others look up to you as a leader. You show honor in protecting and helping others.

- **Average**
  - **Level 4:** You are a hard worker. You strive to accomplish your goals of independence. You deny your own emotional needs.
  - **Level 5:** You need to feel others' support. You forcefully try to control your environment and expect to be obeyed. Your pride keeps you from respecting others.
  - **Level 6:** You use force and intimidation to get your way, sometimes, resorting to threats. You are confrontational. People may resent you for your disrespect.

- **Unhealthy**
  - **Level 7:** You are ruthless, possibly violent. You have no sympathy for others and will sacrifice morals to get your way. You defy any and all authority.

- **Level 8:** You feel invincible, impervious, and omnipotent. You are obsessed with your own power.
- **Level 9:** You are dangerously destructive, potentially sociopathic. Possible Antisocial Personality Disorder.

Subtypes/Instincts

If you are a *social* Eight, you value friendship. You are extremely loyal and willing to make great sacrifices for your friends, and you expect the same from them. You enjoy friendly debates, and you love expressing your opinion in a controversial manner. This trait can be a turn-off to others, but you don't understand why. You enjoy being surrounded by friends and seek others who have strength and independence. If you are psychologically unhealthy, you may often make promises to your friends and not follow through.

As a *sexual* Eight, you can be intense in your relationships. You seek to feel fully alive when you are with your love interests. You want your partner to be strong enough that you can open yourself up, but you may become too domineering in your efforts to form them into the person you want them to be. You enjoy feeling challenged by your partner, but you may become arguments.

Finally, if you are a *self-preservation* Eight, you prioritize the accumulation of resources as a means to independence. You may be a skilled business person. You are resourceful and able to see your way out of most difficult situations, and you are most likely an excellent provider. Others in your household may resent the control you exert over the house resources.

Psychological and Spiritual Growth

An important key to growth as an Eight is to recognize that you do not need to constantly defy the world or view life as a battle of wills. Begin to understand that true strength is found in the ability to open yourself emotionally and express vulnerability. This openness attracts more people.

You have suppressed your innocence because you believe it makes you weak and vulnerable. Learn to reclaim that innocence by appreciating the simplicity and expressing gratitude for small blessings.

Embrace your natural leadership abilities but understand that cooperation will yield more positive results than attempts to bend people to your will. Learn to use less force and appreciate the individualities of people around you.

Notice when you feel vulnerable and out of control, and instead of denying those feelings, accept them. Start by discussing the feelings that make you feel vulnerable with someone you trust. Realize that you most likely will not be met with ridicule or disgust. You are at your most honest and attractive when you can admit to being human. Practice this a little at a time.

Take the experience of a type Eight college campus minister who is learning to harness her overpowering tendencies. Because of Enneagram teachings, she has recently learned to be more aware of her desire to be in control. She explains that, by learning more about her type, she has gained the ability to recognize when she is pushing too hard to advance her own desires.

Thanks to her Enneagram learning and growth experience, this Eight, who is blessed with the strong leadership abilities of most Eights, understands that true leadership means knowing when to give up her agenda for the greater good. She now strives to challenge students on campus to accomplish things for their own good, not just for what she thinks they should do.

Relationships

This section consists of helpful hints *for* Eights in relationships and for people in relationships *with* Eights. These include business relationships, romantic relationships, and parent-child relationships.

Business Relationships FOR *Eights:*
- Learn to respect the individual strengths of others, including those who seem weak.
- Understand that "might makes right" is not necessarily true.
- Decide how much force is needed in each situation.
- Recognize differences between advancing your own agenda and doing what is best for the business.
- Listen to and consider the contributions of others.
- Show appreciation for others.
- Submit to those in authority above you; be respectful when raising concerns or disagreements.
- Be patient, even with those who seem slow or incompetent to you.

Business Relationships WITH *Eights:*
- Make direct eye contact and be assertive.
- Do not disrespect them or try to control them.

- Let them help you get things moving.
- In disagreements, stand up to them and confront them directly.
- Accept their energy but challenge them to rein it in.
- Confront them on destructive or threatening behavior and understand that they may be covering for feelings of vulnerability.

Parenting FOR *Eights:*
- Embrace your instincts to be loyal, protective, involved, and devoted.
- Don't be overprotective; your children need to learn to make mistakes.
- Recognize when you may be too rigid or demanding. Seek the opinion of your co-parent or other parents if you are uncertain. This may feel too vulnerable, but it's good for you!
- Practice patience.

Parenting When Your CHILD *Is an Eight*
- Encourage their independence and fighting spirit if it isn't rebellious or dangerous.
- Don't get in a battle of wills. Explain that you refuse to argue.
- Model submission to authority (the law, your boss, etc.) so your child understands its necessity.
- Watch for manipulation and show that it does not work for you.
- Do not necessarily be concerned if your child is a loner, but encourage him or her to look for things they appreciate and admire in their peers.
- Be a model of expressing vulnerability and emotional openness. Reward this with respect and affection.

Romantic Relationships FOR *Eights:*
- Listen to your partner's point of view.
- Tell your partner regularly what you are thankful for them being with you.
- Get feedback for how forcefully you come across.
- Learn to open emotionally. Start in small ways and build.
- Explain when you don't feel safe and allow for reassurance.
- Find an activity (separate from your partner) where you can safely release the anger that is kept within you.
- Practice patience.
- Resist the urge to be possessive.

Romantic Relationships WITH *Eights:*
- Notice any time they open emotionally and reward this with respect and affection.
- Show appreciation for times when they make sacrifices for you, show extra loyalty or commitment.
- Be direct with them when you have anything to discuss.
- Stand up to them when you feel they seem to be controlling or talking down to you.
- Remind them they don't have to carry the weight of the world on their shoulders.

Chapter 5: Type 9 – The Peacemaker

Type 9 Checklist: *Ask yourself if the following statements are true for you.*

- You are generally patient and easygoing.
- You are receptive and agreeable when hearing the ideas of others.
- You think of yourself as uncomplicated and contented.
- You have been accused of being unrealistic in the way that you idealize people and the way that the world should work.
- You are not usually self-conscious.
- You are a steady and supportive friend.
- You can be very imaginative and creative.
- You prefer to "keep the peace" rather than show when you are upset.
- You sometimes escape into distraction to deal with tension or neglect.
- Occasionally, you have "blown up" after absorbing too much abuse and holding it in for too long.
- You have difficulty standing up for yourself and voicing your own feelings.
- You prefer to keep your life simple and stick to a few close friends and family members.
- You want to believe the best in people and hope for the best for yourself.
- You would rather avoid a problem than confront it head-on.
- You make an excellent mediator in conflicts.

If you can relate to more than half of the above statements, chances are that you are a Nine or you have a strong Nine wing. Keep reading to learn more about your type!

Core Belief

The belief that drives your behavior is that you have to always go with the flow or blend in so that you feel valued and loved. You believe that the world would be a better place if everyone just treated each other more respectfully and tried to get along.

Avoidance: *Conflict*

You avoid the discomfort of conflict at all costs. You fear "rocking the boat" because it may lead to loss and separation, and as a result, you often deny your needs and desires.

Trap: *Being Temperate*

You can become so preoccupied with making peace and/or avoiding conflict that you end up repressing powerful feelings within you.

Idealization: *I am harmonious.*

By appearing harmonious and keeping the peace, you protect yourself from the pain of being dismissed or hurt by the ones you love.

Defense Mechanism: *Narcotization*

Narcotization is "numbing out" to deal with negative feelings, and it is a common defense mechanism in Nines.

You may use TV or other technology, repetitive thinking patterns, comfort food, alcohol, or even drugs to stop feeling any painful emotions. Even seemingly productive activity can be a type of narcotization if it keeps you from facing your emotions.

Passion: *Sloth* (*Disengagement*)

You pay a large price for the relaxed, harmonious image that you project. Because you spend so much of your emotional energy suppressing anger and frustration with other people (and with yourself), you feel fatigued much of the time. You feel that you have no more energy left to spend, so you end up being disengaged from life. This sloth is not necessarily a quality of laziness, even if it may appear so to others.

Description

You seek to achieve and maintain a sense of peace in your world, both externally and internally. You prefer to create harmony in your environment.

You are usually able to see multiple points of view in a conflict. This makes you an excellent mediator, which people value in your personal life and in the business world.

Sometimes, you have trouble staying on task or prioritizing what needs to be done. You're an excellent "big picture" thinker, but you may need help seeing the details. Short-term objectives work best for you.

You struggle to focus on disturbing or negative issues, and you just want to avoid them instead. Dealing with conflict in your environment has been learned as a child by being undemanding and withdrawing. As an adult, you are un-demanding and non-judgmental, and these qualities draw people to you and make you a supportive friend.

As a member of the *Instinctive Triad*, you have issues with anger, which you deal with by denying it and focusing on creating peace for the other people in your life instead. You are usually unaware of any repressed anger inside you, but sometimes, it comes out explosively. If you are surrounded by tense conditions or frustrated with the behavior of people around you, you may eventually reach a boiling point and erupt. Afterward, you hope to just keep going as if "everything is ok."

One of the best qualities about you is your optimism. You want to believe in the best about other people and hope for the best for yourself. You may work hard to accomplish this end, or you may just focus on keeping your life uncomplicated. People often disappoint you, and if you are in an unhealthy state of mind, you may become fatalistic about life in general.

Wings

The personalities to either side of you on the Enneagram are Eight, the Challenger, and One, the Reformer. A Nine with a stronger Eight-Wing has been labeled "The Referee" by some, and a Nine with a stronger One-Wing has been labeled "The Dreamer." Look at the chapters on these two personalities to decide if you identify more strongly with one of these wings.

Directions of Integration and Disintegration

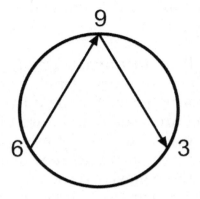

Your direction of integration is toward type Three, the Achiever. When you are emotionally healthy, you exhibit some of the qualities of a healthy Three. You have believed that your own perspective is unimportant, but if you work through this belief, you can see that others value you fully and want to hear your thoughts and feelings. You understand that you hold intrinsic value, and you begin to develop your own interests and talents so you can share them with the world.

If you are less emotionally healthy but still, in secure conditions, you display average Three traits. You may be able to show your value to a few trusted people who are close to you. Under secure circumstances, you deal with stress by being extra productive as a way of trying to prove your worth and impress others.

Your direction of disintegration is towards type Six, the Loyalist. Your first reaction to stressful situations is emotional detachment, but eventually, you may become irritable. Although complaining is typically out of character to you, you may begin vocalizing your displeasure and blaming others. If the stress continues, you become even more anxious and reactive.

Levels of Development

The following is a very brief breakdown of your levels of development as a Nine, so you can begin to recognize your psychological health and warning signs that you may have some work to do.

- **Healthy**
  - **Level 1 (at your best):** You can be present and aware of your own emotions. Your contentment does not depend on the harmony of those around you because you are connected to your inner self. You can form deeper bonds with others.
  - **Level 2:** You are stable and serene. Others are drawn to your accepting nature. Your life is simple and you are genuinely good-natured.
  - **Level 3:** Others seek out your meditation abilities. Your strengths are your optimism, calming influence, and communication skills.

- **Average**
  - **Level 4:** You go along with the desires of others, even when contradictory to your desires. You believe the best in others. Your fear of conflict keeps you from acknowledging your needs.
  - **Level 5:** Because you don't want to be affected by conflict, you disengage from

much of life. You walk away from problems and escape into your own thoughts.

- o **Level 6**: You try to keep other people happy by minimizing problems. You feel resigned to the fact that nothing can improve. You are fairly withdrawn and inactive.

- **Unhealthy**
  - o **Level 7:** You are emotionally undeveloped and have highly repressed anger. You remove yourself from problems because you feel that you're unable to face them.
  - o **Level 8:** You numb yourself to the extent that you may no longer be able to fully function.
  - o **Level 9:** You are severely dissociated and unaware of reality. Possible multiple personalities, Schizoid, and Dependent personality disorders.

Subtypes/Instincts

If you are a *social* Nine, you are more active and outgoing than most Nines. You like to participate in community causes and organizations. Even if you are heavily involved in a group, you manage to be unaffected by conflicts within the group, because you are friendly but not deeply involved with others in the group. You keep busy with your participation in a cause, but you are not necessarily internally motivated. You may be easily distracted.

As a *sexual* Nine, you seek someone to share your sense of ease and gentleness. You can be highly sensual and imaginative. The idea of a special union with someone is attractive to you, but you fear to lose your identity because of your inability to express your wants and needs. You may hold back from a relationship and not fully show up emotionally. This can create the tensions that you desperately want to avoid.

Finally, if you are a *self-preservation* Nine, you seek comfort and familiarity above other priorities. You value your alone time and do not appreciate changes to your environment. You may struggle with inactivity and overeating, or you may be very rigid with your diet. Two of your most positive characteristics are your common sense and patience.

Psychological and Spiritual Growth

As a Nine, you value other people more than you value yourself. Take time to reflect on attributes about yourself that are valuable and desirable. Appreciate what you bring to the table.

When you want to complain, try to determine what hidden want or need you have repressed. Would it be so terrible to express this want or need? You may fear criticism and not being taken seriously, so start small with your self-assertion. Practice small assertions until you are comfortable enough to express yourself in something more important, and then keep practicing!

By denying your feelings and devaluing your own opinion, you create disunion within yourself. You will not experience true union with others until you have union within yourself. Asserting yourself is not aggressive; it is positive and will cause others to respect you more.

For many Nines, mindfulness meditation is helpful. Meditation can take many forms, so research effective meditation methods for your type. The most useful meditations for Nines include recognizing and accepting emotions, valuing yourself as much as you value others, and discovering your own intentions and purposes.

Notice physical sensations of discomfort in your body when you encounter conflict. Instead of fleeing, remind yourself that it is naturally occurring and learn to deal with the conflict constructively.

Recognize that some conflicts and pain in the world are unavoidable. You have the gift of mediation, and you can use this gift to genuinely bring more peace to others.

Reflect on a story of growth from fellow Nine. She has become aware that she tends to support other people's plans while sacrificing her own plans. She knows now that it is critical for her to acknowledge her own wants and needs, even when she feels bad for doing so.

This Nine admits that she has trouble getting started with positive action at times because she is often tempted to sit and let life pass her by. She also has trouble concentrating on her own priorities, because she is so used to letting other people's priorities be more important. The habit of letting go of her own desires to "keep the peace" is deeply ingrained in her, and she is used to keeping any anger locked deep inside herself. Sometimes that anger comes exploding out, with damaging effects to herself and others. But now, thanks to learning about herself through teachings from the Enneagram, she is starting to get help.

Through the Enneagram, this woman learned to get help through something called bioenergetic work, which is a type of therapy accomplished through body movement techniques. The body positions held in a bioenergetic session are designed to help participants get in touch with their emotions through physical movement. This particular Nine has discovered her own desires and needs through group sessions in bioenergetics. She has even learned to express her anger safely.

She now feels empowered to pursue her own interests in music, and she finds that her music feels much more authentic thanks to her Enneagram and bioenergetics work. Through a new connection with her true self, she now feels more alive than she has ever felt!

If you are a Nine who is constantly squelching your own needs and wants to keep the peace around you, or if you are keeping anger locked inside yourself, it is our hope that you will continue to learn about your emotions and desires. Find ways to get in touch with them and express them so that you, too, can feel alive and whole.

Relationships

This final section consists of lists with helpful hints *for* Nines in relationships and for people in relationships *with* Nines. These include business relationships, romantic relationships, and parent-child relationships.

Business Relationships FOR *Nines:*
- When speaking to a group, plan what you will say ahead of time and get to the point quickly.
- Stay present and prioritize what needs to be done in each moment.
- Learn to keep to an agenda with deadlines.

- Remember that conflicts are sometimes inevitable; breathe and find constructive ways to deal with conflict.
- Work on making your valuable opinions known.
- Do not be too accommodating to your associates; show that you have a backbone and firmly stand your ground when necessary.

Business Relationships WITH *Nines:*
- Remind them of their personal needs and rights.
- Nines are good at seeing the big picture but need help structuring steps of how to reach the goal. Set short-term objectives for them.
- Ask them for cooperation instead of trying to push them around.
- Be accepting of their personality while challenging them and helping them to take risks.
- Remind them that saying "No" does not always start a conflict.
- Listen to them well and avoid coming on too strong or acting impatient.

Parenting FOR *Nines:*
- You are good at being supportive, kind, and warm. Keep it up!
- Avoid being overly permissive. Accept that you cannot always make your child happy.
- You have to set limits for your child to keep them safe and help them grow into a responsible adult.
- Don't take it personally when your child is upset with you.
- Recognize how you would like your child to behave and remember it's ok to assert these expectations.

Parenting When Your CHILD *Is A Nine*
- Make sure they know you notice and value them.

- Ask how they are feeling during and after conflicts in your home.
- Remind them it is ok to be angry. Help them find healthy outlets for emotions.
- Listen to any concerns they have and do not come across as overly critical.
- Model healthy ways of resolving a conflict.

Romantic Relationships FOR *Nines:*
- Recognize that you have aggression, anxieties, and other feelings you must deal with to have healthy relationships. Get things out in the open instead of suppressing them.
- Express wants and needs clearly.
- Work on staying present and being an active participant in your relationship.
- Find a healthy solo outlet for emotions, like regular exercise.
- Stand up for yourself if you are feeling controlled or ignored.

Romantic Relationships WITH *Nines:*

- Avoid creating pressure, getting impatient, or coming on too strong.
- Know what they need and want by asking them. Give them time to discern the answer.
- Tell them it's ok to say "no," especially if you sense they are reluctant about something.
- Share physical activities, like exercising or cooking together.
- Support them to act when they want to do something.
- Show physical affection. It helps open them up to their feelings.

- Discuss but don't confront.
- Compliment the way they look.
- Share in their enjoyment of life.

Chapter 6: Type 1 – The Reformer

Type 1 Checklist: *Ask yourself if the following statements are true for you.*

- You feel personally obligated to improve yourself and the world.
- You are extremely responsible, sensible, conscientious, and ethical.
- You have a sense of discipline that comes from within.
- You tend to think that nothing is ever quite good enough.
- You are continually aware of flaws in yourself, others, and situations.
- You often feel guilty for being unable to achieve perfection. You also feel guilty for your anger against an imperfect world.
- You follow the rules and expect others to do so as well.
- You are driven and ambitious, sometimes, workaholic.
- You are good at getting things done.
- You are a loyal, responsible, and capable partner and friend.
- You are often tense and have a hard time relaxing.
- You have natural organizational skills.
- You tend to be aware of how your actions might affect future situations.
- You have a deep feeling of purpose for your life and you have a fairly good idea of what that purpose might be.
- You have deep convictions about right and wrong.

If you can relate to more than half of the above statements, you are probably a type One or have a strong One wing. Keep reading to learn more about your type!

Core Belief

The belief that drives your behavior is that you must gain worthiness and love by being as good and perfect as possible. You feel that you need to work diligently towards improving an imperfect world.

Avoidance: *Imperfection*

You avoid making mistakes or appearing wrong at all costs, even though you are acutely aware of your own imperfections and have a strong sense of never being good enough.

Trap: *Making Things Right*

You can get caught up in your attempts to achieve perfection. Your inner criticism and anger at an imperfect world are very damaging to you.

Idealization: *I am good and right.*

This is the image that you wish to project to the world. Although your strong sense of right and wrong aide you in seeking justice, you hold yourself and others to impossible standards in which simple human mistakes are "bad." Your fear is being wrong because this would make you unworthy.

Defense Mechanism: *Reaction Formation*

Reaction formation is a defense mechanism in which any unacceptable emotions are supposedly overcome by an exaggerated display of the exact opposite behavior. You see your anger as a "bad" emotion, so you turn it inward while maintaining an outward appearance of self-control and purposeful action.

Passion: *Anger/Resentment*

As a member of the *Instinctive Triad,* you struggle with anger, even though you view anger as a "bad" emotion. You turn it inwards against yourself; your harsh inner self-critic constantly berates you for your imperfections. Your feelings of having higher standards than everyone else makes you feel irritated and resentful.

Description

You are goal-oriented and concerned with *how* you accomplish your goals. You feel that you must achieve results while still adhering to strict ethical standards. Second-best is unacceptable.

You have most likely felt a strong sense of purpose in your life since childhood. More importantly, you have a good idea of exactly what that purpose might be, and you strive to accomplish that purpose.

Your ethical standards give you strong convictions of social justice. Consequently, you are often committed to causes as a part of your mission to improve the world. Your many positive traits include attention to detail and ability to be objective and fair. You are very principled, valuing integrity, reliable, and responsible. You have a natural talent for organization.

You are used to constantly judging yourself, and your internal dialogue contains phrases such as "I should" and "I must." Unfortunately, you feel that you will never live up to your own standards and you can be deeply unhappy with yourself as a result.

You often do not realize when you appear impatient to others, even though you try to hide and control this emotion. You rarely express anger without thinking it through thoroughly and presenting the offender with a list of past experiences – "proof" that you are right. You have an especially hard time accepting even the most constructive of criticism because you view it as evidence of failure.

Wings

The personalities to either side of you on the Enneagram are Nine, the Peacemaker, and Two, the Helper. A One with a stronger Nine-Wing has been labeled "The Idealist" by some, and a One with a stronger Two-Wing has been labeled "The Advocate." Look at the chapters on these two personalities to decide if you identify more strongly with one of them.

Directions of Integration and Disintegration

Your direction of integration is towards Seven, the Enthusiast. When you are emotionally healthy, you can exhibit some of the qualities of a healthy Seven. As you work through your rigid need for perfection, you become less strict and experience a sense of freedom from obligation. As you accept yourself, you become grateful for the differences of those around you.

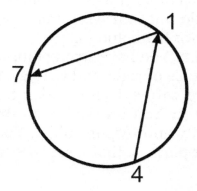

If you are less emotionally healthy but still, in secure conditions, you display the traits of an average Seven. This means that you may be less inhibited and express emotions around people you trust. You may allow yourself to express some of your own needs, which may come across as selfish.

Your direction of disintegration is towards Four, the Individualist. If you feel that you have much higher standards than those around you, you become resentful, forcing yourself to do the work that you believe others will not. You become depressed and disillusioned, leading you to isolate and possibly indulge in behaviors that you rigidly kept from allowing yourself before, like eating "forbidden" foods.

Levels of Development

The following is a very brief breakdown of your levels of development as a One, so you recognize your psychological health and warning signs of deterioration:

- **Healthy**
    - o **Level 1 (at your best):** You accept the imperfections of yourself and others; you are realistic but still wise and discerning. You strive for truth and justice.
    - o **Level 2:** You have strong moral convictions and sense of right and wrong. You try to be mature, rational, and moderate.
    - o **Level 3:** You are fair and ethical, valuing integrity and responsibility. You strive for a higher purpose that you sense for yourself.

- **Average**
    - o **Level 4:** You are involved in social causes, feeling it is up to you to affect change. You are dissatisfied with the world you live in.
    - o **Level 5:** You fear mistakes, making you rigid with feelings and impulses. Possibly workaholic due to obligation.
    - o **Level 6**: You are extremely critical of yourself and others. You are often impatient and dissatisfied with other people.

- **Unhealthy**
    - o **Level 7:** You are self-righteous and intolerant. Only you know the best way; you judge others severely.
    - o **Level 8:** You become obsessive about proclaiming others' imperfections.
    - o **Level 9:** You condemn others and try to punish them. You may be severely depressed and/or suicidal. Possibly Obsessive-Compulsive or Depressive personality disorder.

Subtypes/Instincts

If you are a *social* One, you take local and world issues personally and spend your energy attempting to make others care as much as you do. You can't just talk about what's wrong with the world, you need to *do* something about it! You can become so heavily involved in your causes that you cannot develop much of a social life. Although you lack balance in this way, your convictions are admirably strong, and you contribute greatly to the community.

If you are a *sexual* One, you can become a perfectionist about your romantic relationships. Your critical nature makes it difficult to find an acceptable partner, so you get excited when you meet someone who seems to share your values and goals. You may idealize this person and worry that you aren't good enough for them. You may also struggle with being overly critical of your partner. Strengths that you bring to intimate relationships are a strong sense of commitment and devotion to continual growth and improvement.

Finally, if you are a *self-preservation* One, you can be very rigid and even militant about the way you run your household. You have well-formed and firm ideas about nutrition, budgeting, exercise, and maintaining order. You feel that keeping order and cleanliness, along with careful planning, will help ensure your survival somehow. You may become very passionate about preserving your family's health.

Psychological and Spiritual Growth Tips

As a One, you need a sense of balance and compassion to temper your rigid need for perfection, which is unnatural and impossible. Learn to give yourself grace, treat yourself with compassion, and accept yourself as you are. Slowly start to tune out the inner critical voice and allow yourself to relax and take time to do something strictly for enjoyment.

Instead of automatically turning your anger inwards, pause, and question what person, place, or thing you are finding unacceptable. Tell yourself that everything is ok as it is, and mistakes are a natural part of learning and growing. Accept others' imperfections as a part of their beauty and do the same for yourself!

Notice and accept your natural desires and emotions. Instead of dismissing or judging them, observe them and get in the practice of expressing them or writing them down.

You have trouble with physical relaxation, so now learn to allow yourself to feel pleasure while breathing. This may feel uncomfortable at first but take it slow and keep trying. The important part is to relax and inhale slowly, then exhale gently. Do some further research on breathing exercises for tension release.

Perhaps, you can relate to the experience of another One, who felt as if she was being strangled by a compulsion to constantly prove she was worthy. She learned to work hard, put on the façade of being perfect, and not let her feelings show, because she felt that was the only way she could be accepted and loved. Throughout her life, her false ego forced her to different college degrees, careers and anything else possible to escape her fears of being unloved or unacceptable. But she felt that nothing worked, and she was in deep pain.

This One goes on to describe how she was introduced to the Enneagram, and eventually, after a particularly painful rejection, she experienced transformation. She says that she finally learned to lower her defenses and be vulnerable for the first time in her life. She finally realized that she could never be perfect and she needed to rely on a Higher Power to get in touch with her authentic self.

She found serenity by following the blueprints to self-discovery provided by the Enneagram. It was only the beginning of the journey, but by getting started on this journey she found a way to accept and embrace her whole self, even the parts that were less than perfect. By allowing herself to feel helpless, she was able to let go of control and finally trust.

If you are a One who feels stifled and suffocated by the compulsion to be perfect, hopefully, you will also be able to recognize that there is another way. You can be vulnerable and admit your shortcomings. By being human and expressing your fears and emotions, you can learn to trust and feel whole.

Relationships

This section consists of lists with helpful hints *for* Ones in relationships and for people in relationships *with* Ones. These include business relationships, romantic relationships, and parent-child relationships.

Business Relationships FOR *Ones:*
- Use your self-discipline to accomplish your goals but try not to become upset when others aren't trying as hard as you.
- Instead of badgering, try gently encouraging others.

- Look for value in others; appreciate them for their unique qualities.
- Appreciate errors, mistakes, and imperfections as differences.
- Admit mistakes and practice acceptance when you hear constructive criticism.
- Use your sense of ethics to be discerning about right and wrong without judging.
- Point out the positive.

Business Relationships WITH *Ones:*
- Speak respectfully and try not to make them feel foolish.
- Make small gestures like being on time and giving proper instructions.
- Admit errors immediately to clear the air and prevent resentment.
- Notice and compliment specific things like dependability and punctuality.
- Avoid power struggles and work cooperatively.
- Demonstrate how two "right" ways can co-exist.
- Avoid making agreements that you cannot keep.
- Ask them to be direct with anger.
- Use their ideas to help you see how things can be improved.
- Remind them to share responsibility with others.

Parenting FOR *Ones:*
- You are good at teaching responsibility and moral values. Keep it up!
- Allow silliness and expression of a wide range of emotions.
- If you must discipline firmly, do it with love and be sure your child knows they are forgiven. Explain that they need to be held accountable.

- Remember they are children, and they will be messy and imperfect. Embrace their beautiful imperfections.
- Be gentle and clear when expressing expectations.

Parenting When Your CHILD Is A One
- Model acceptance of imperfections and admit your own mistakes.
- Give grace freely, because they likely are harshly criticizing themselves on the inside.
- Praise responsibility and conscientious behavior.
- Affirm that it's ok to make mistakes and ask for help.
- Check in with their emotions. Ask if they are angry when they make mistakes and give time and space to express that anger.
- Encourage them to try new things, even if they fear failure.

Romantic Relationships FOR Ones:
- Appreciate differences between you and your partner.
- Express worries but try to laugh at yourself when you get uptight.
- Tolerate and enjoy your partner's point of view.
- Practice forgiveness toward yourself and your partner.
- Talk openly about any anger you may be feeling toward yourself.
- Give yourself an outlet to release tension and frustration you may be feeling toward the other person.

Romantic Relationships WITH Ones:
- Bring fun activities and laughter to your relationship.

- Help them be less critical of themselves and accepting of their mistakes.
- Remind them to share their frustrations.
- Take your share of responsibilities so that they don't do all the work.
- Reassure them that they are valued the way they are.
- Compliment achievements.
- Tell them you value their advice.
- Apologize if you have been inconsiderate and model admitting your mistakes with ease.

The Feeling Triad
(Types 2, 3 & 4)

Chapter 7: Type 2 – The Helper

Type 2 Checklist: *Ask yourself if the following statements are true for you.*

- You care deeply about other people and the details of their lives.
- You feel best about yourself when you are meaningfully engaged with others.
- You genuinely enjoy supporting other people with attention and care.
- You are especially good at remembering important details about other people.
- You try to do nice things so others will think well of you.
- You have had trouble with not taking enough care of yourself.
- Sometimes, people have accused you of having "boundary issues" or being a "people-pleaser."
- You sometimes struggle to find self-worth outside of your relationships.
- You are very sensitive to and perceptive about others' feelings
- You have a good sense of humor, and you are fun-loving.
- You can become upset when others don't sense your needs as well as you sense their needs.
- You genuinely enjoy seeing the best in others.

- You fear rejection because it makes you feel worthless.
- You are drawn toward jobs that revolve around helping people.
- You tend to be generous and considerate.

If you can relate to more than half of the above statements, you're probably a Two or you have a strong Two wing. Keep reading to learn more about your type!

Core Belief

The belief that drives your behavior is that you must give fully to others to be loved. At your core, you believe that you are only worthwhile and loveable because you are loving and needed.

Avoidance: *Your Own Needs*

You would rather help others and meet their needs than focus on your own wants and needs because you believe that doing so would make you appear needy. As a result, you deny and avoid any personal needs that you may have.

Trap: *Being of Service*

There is potential for you to be so caught up in your obsession with being of service that you thoroughly exhaust yourself. You can be extremely busy with all your commitments, but when someone new asks for help, you still say yes.

Idealization: *I am helpful.*

This is the image that you try to project to the world because you believe it is what makes you worthwhile. You fear that if you were not able to help others, you would be seen negatively in the eyes of others and ultimately be rejected.

Defense Mechanism: *Repression*

Repression is keeping some feeling out of conscious awareness. For you, repression keeps your own needs out of the picture. You have an incredible ability to sense and fulfill the needs of others, but you use this to avoid being present and aware of your own needs.

Passion: *Pride*

You run the risk of thinking that you, and you alone, can help and/or save certain people. When pride is active in you, you are trying to be appreciated and loved by appearing selfless and giving.

Description

You are the kind of person who remembers everyone's birthday, stays up late to take care of someone or drives across town to deliver food to a sick friend. You are warm and emotional, and you devote much energy to personal relationships. People appreciate that you notice and think of "the little things."

You may excel in a profession that involves helping others, like teaching or nursing. You know how to make a home comfortable and inviting. If you have a family, you are absolutely in your element when caring for a sick child or spouse. Not all Twos are in a helping profession or have a family to take care of, though. You may not even recognize the extent of your involvement in assisting others.

As selfless as you appear on the outside, you thrive on feeling helpful and needed, so your self-sacrifice is not without ulterior motives. Being needed makes you feel important and being helpful makes you feel virtuous. Reading this may be a surprise to you, because you may have thoroughly convinced yourself of your own selflessness.

You may remember times when you became resentful because someone didn't thank you or show appreciation for your assistance. You may feel entitled to some thanks; after all, you worked hard and deserve some gratitude.

Because you spend so much time and energy helping others, you often forget to take care of yourself. Or you may feel that you don't really have many needs. Or when asked, you may not even know what you want and need! This is not uncommon for Twos. However, you do have wants and needs of your own, and if you don't take the time to attend to them you can get utterly burned out.

Friends or family members might say that you are a "people-pleaser." This means that you try to get people to like you by doing things for them. The reason for this isn't that you are selfish. It's because deep down, you feel that you have no worth of your own unless you are helpful and needed.

Wings

The personalities to either side of you on the Enneagram are One, the Reformer, and Three, the Achiever. A Two with a stronger One-Wing has been labeled "The Servant" by some, and a Two with a stronger Three-Wing has been labeled "The Host/Hostess." Look at the chapters on these two personalities to decide if you identify more strongly with one of these.

Directions of Integration and Disintegration

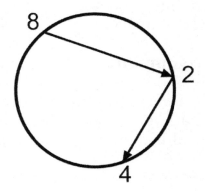

Your direction of integration is toward type Four, the Individualist. This means that when you are emotionally healthy, you exhibit some qualities of a healthy Four. As you become willing to express your needs and hidden emotions, you learn to accept yourself. You find that you can support others in a healthy way, without trying to get them to like you. You also begin to be able to accept your own humanity and so you achieve more intimacy with others in healthy relationships.

If you are less emotionally healthy but still, in secure conditions, you display the traits of an average Four. When you are feeling sure of yourself, you may be able to admit your needs and feelings to a few people that you are comfortable with. Since this is rare for you, you might become moody, selfish, and over-sensitive at these times.

Your disintegration is towards Eight, the Challenger. You feel stressed when you feel that your helpfulness is not noticed or appreciated, and this is when disintegration happens. You display characteristics of average to unhealthy Eights, meaning that you act out in bossy and controlling ways to make people notice you. At particularly bad times, you might even become extremely confrontational and angry.

Levels of Development

The following is a very brief breakdown of your levels of development as a Two, so you can begin to recognize your psychological health and warning signs that of emotional deterioration.

- **Healthy**
    - **Level 1 (at your best):** You realize you're allowed to take care of yourself. You love and are loved unconditionally. You believe good things can happen without your help. You are humble and charitable.
    - **Level 2:** You are thoughtful, warm-hearted, and sincere in compassion. You are genuinely concerned about others' needs.
    - **Level 3:** You value service but also take care of yourself. You generously encourage, love, and nurture others.

- **Average**
  - ○ **Level 4:** "People pleasing" starts. You have good intentions on the surface; underneath, you want to be liked. You can resort to the flattery of others.
  - ○ **Level 5:** You feel a strong desire to be needed; manipulate others to make them depend on you. You are prideful as you remind others of how caring you are. Can be intrusive in your "helpfulness."
  - ○ **Level 6**: You feel others take you for granted and owe you recognition. You try to instill guilt in others for not caring about your needs.

- **Unhealthy**
  - ○ **Level 7:** You project the image of having done nothing wrong while manipulating others into feeling sympathy. You deceive yourself about your motives, believing you are unselfish.
  - ○ **Level 8:** You are controlling and feel entitled to receive repayment for all you have done. You coerce others to give you what they owe.
  - ○ **Level 9:** You feel victimized, so you rationalize any manipulative behavior. Possible Histrionic Personality Disorder or Factitious Disorder.

Subtypes/Instincts

If you are a *social* Two, you wish to be friends with as many people as possible. You make yourself indispensable to any group that you are in by becoming intricately involved in the lives of its members. You offer a sympathetic listening ear to anyone in a crisis, you dispense advice, and offer support to as many people as possible. You like helping important people. You are probably very outgoing and excellent at remembering other people's names. You may struggle with becoming over-committed due to your inability to say "no."

If you are a *sexual* Two, you crave to be as close as possible with your partner. You find out about their preferences, wants, needs, and hobbies, and then do everything you can to provide those things to them. You focus much of your sole attention and affection on a mate, making them want to spend more time with you. You are often the initiator of physical touch. If you are psychologically unhealthy, you may become obsessed with a significant other and not be able to let go of them.

Finally, as *self-preservation* Two, you nurture and take care of those around you to fulfill your need for love and satisfaction with yourself. You hope others will return the favor by taking care of you, but you don't know how to ask for what you want or need. All you can do is drop hints and keep hoping, but sometimes, the others never reciprocate. Because your own needs are not met, you may overindulge in food, alcohol, or other addictive substances because on some level, you feel you "deserve" to indulge. This is dangerous, but you may not know how else to deal with your feelings of loneliness and rejection.

Psychological and Spiritual Growth

Your growth as a Two depends on your recognition that you can care for yourself and others at the same time. In fact, if you really wish to be helpful and nurturing to others, you absolutely *must* care for your own spiritual and physical needs first. Only then will you be in the best possible condition to attend to the needs of those around you.

Similarly, you only reach the emotional intimacy that you crave with others by first recognizing and expressing your own emotions. As a member of the *Feeling Triad*, your emotional issues center around shame. You are ashamed of your own needs and unpleasant emotions, but you need to become comfortable with the fact that it is normal and healthy to have unpleasant emotions and to have needs of your own.

This change cannot happen overnight, of course. Start by reflecting on how you are truly feeling and what needs are not being met. As you begin to be able to recognize your emotions and needs, try voicing them to someone you trust and are very close to. As you learn that you will not be rejected for expressing yourself, you will realize that your worth does not come from denying your needs or constantly being useful to others; it comes from within you.

If you are over-committed, realize that it would be so much more beneficial for everyone if you were to focus on one or two causes or groups that you feel most passionate about. You'll have more time to care for yourself and be healthier as a result. A healthier, more grounded you can give to those you care about with more energy and love.

Consider the experience of a Two who, after experiencing self-discovery through the Enneagram, began to reflect on former past relationships. He realized that he had arrogantly felt that his significant others and close friends truly needed his advice, love, help, and wisdom. Although he was not meaning to be manipulative and he felt that he was being sincere, he began to realize that he was using these other people to meet his own needs.

This Two states that he gravitated towards others whom he thought he could help by being understanding and helping others to understand them. He wanted to be the one and only person who could meet another person's needs. He found his self-worth in being needed and felt panic and desperation when he felt that someone no longer needed him. He would even take great measures to become what he thought someone needed him to be.

Unfortunately, these intense relationships often took a nasty turn when this Two realized that he was being controlled and manipulated. He would feel trapped in the role that he had created for himself, and then he would want to be free.

Finally, after acquiring self-knowledge through the Enneagram and undergoing years of therapy, he now realizes that he had deep rage, loneliness, and sadness inside himself. He now feels able to express his own needs without feeling at risk of being abandoned. He knows that by meeting his own needs he is lifting a burden off of other people (the burden he placed on them by trying to meet his needs through helping them). He feels that he now is moving closer to becoming his authentic self.

If any of that Two's struggles sound like your own, now you know that you are not alone and you can find freedom! Expressing your needs and caring for yourself do *not* make you more likely to be abandoned. In fact, self-care will make you a more genuine and grounded version of yourself, and people will be even more drawn to you than before.

Relationships

This section consists of lists with helpful hints *for* Twos in relationships and for people in relationships *with* Twos. These include business relationships, romantic relationships, and parent-child relationships.

Business Relationships FOR *Twos:*
- Recognize when you are overdoing things or becoming too intrusive/involved and step back.
- Try doing something the way *you* want to do it but have been too ashamed or fearful to suggest.
- Instead of jumping in and offering to help, wait to be asked sometimes.
- Try helping because you *want* to help, not because you are seeking approval.
- Take time to fulfill your needs.
- Practice saying no.
- Tell truths honestly without a positive spin.

Business Relationships WITH *Twos:*
- Be gentle with criticism.
- Tell them that you appreciate their contributions; be specific.
- In conflicts, ask them to take responsibility for getting what they want rather than indirectly blaming others.
- Connect with them in valuing partnership, personal contact, and warmth.
- Don't assume that they will be the one to help when a volunteer is needed. Ask others to help before coming to them.
- Help them set boundaries with anyone that takes advantage of them.
- Help them take time out for themselves.

Parenting FOR *Twos:*
- You are good at listening, encouraging, and loving unconditionally. Keep it up!
- Keep having fun and being playful with your children.
- Don't second-guess everything you do. Everyone makes mistakes in parenting and most mistakes are not detrimental.
- Your protective nature can be a good thing, but let your children try new things, face fears, and make mistakes.
- Don't be hurt when your children do not remember to thank you.
- Resist the urge to guilt-trip your children.

Parenting When Your CHILD *Is A Two*
- Model expressing your needs and feelings politely.
- Give criticism gently and in the form of suggestion.
- Show appreciation for the help that they give and be specific.
- Give attention to them generously, so they don't feel the need to act a certain way to get your attention.
- Encourage them to talk about their feelings and to spend time alone doing something they enjoy.

Romantic Relationships FOR Twos:
- Choose relationships where your authentic self is appreciated and celebrated.
- Pay attention to your own needs instead of constantly immersing yourself in the other person's needs.
- Spend time alone doing something healthy that meets your needs.
- Practice expressing your needs and wants.

- Don't manipulate with guilt if you feel unappreciated. Instead, ask yourself what need you have that hasn't been met.
- Don't do things for the other person to get more love—just do them because you love them.

Romantic Relationships WITH *Twos:*
- Reassure them that they are interesting to you and that you love them.
- Be gentle with any criticism.
- Share plenty of fun times.
- Take an interest in their problems; don't take advantage of their nature by letting them constantly focus on your problems.
- Let them know they are special to you.
- Tell them you're glad to be seen with them.
- Encourage them to take time for themselves.
- Ask them what they need and how they are feeling.

Chapter 8: Type 3 – The Achiever

Type 3 Checklist: *Ask yourself if the following statements are true for you.*

- You want to be the best at everything you do.
- You are willing to do whatever it takes to stand out as the best.
- You are goal-oriented.
- You have trouble understanding people who are not as motivated as you to pursue dreams.
- You have learned to adapt easily to achieve your goals.
- You value efficiency and effectiveness.
- You tend to brush aside your own feelings to get things done.
- You often push yourself too hard.
- When you are struggling, you try to convince others that you are fine.
- As a child, you learned to perform in ways that would earn praise and positive attention.
- It is important to you that you appear successful to others.
- You are very competitive and love winning.
- You are good at appearing confident and optimistic, even when you do not feel that way.
- You can become short-tempered when you face the possibility of failure.

If you can relate to more than half of the above statements, you probably are a Three or you have a strong Three wing. Keep reading to learn more about your type!

Core Belief

The belief that drives your behavior is the world values winners, and you must achieve success to be worthwhile and loved. You believe that worth comes from doing, not simply being.

Avoidance: *Failure*

You have a deep fear of failure because success is worthless in your eyes. You avoid sitting around "doing nothing" because that is almost the equivalent of failure to you. If you were ever unable to accomplish anything, you feel that you would have no value.

Trap: *Achieving (Efficiency)*

You can be so caught up in your goal of doing everything as well as possible and as quickly as possible that the goal controls you. You can become so alienated from yourself that you don't know what your desires, feelings, or interests are.

Idealization: *I am successful/I am a winner.*

You wish to present an image of success in the world. You thrive on the approval and applause that you get from this image, and you find your identity and self-worth in achievement.

Defense Mechanism: *Identification*

Identification is a defense mechanism in which you unconsciously take characteristics of another person into your own personality and sense of self. When you feel threatened by perceived or possibly real failure, you tend to identify with someone that you admire and see as successful. In doing this, you avoid failure and maintain a self-image of success.

Passion: *Vanity (Deceit)*

You hide any inner qualities that you feel are inadequate and strive to only display qualities that you believe a "winner" has. Your passion of vanity or deceit starts with you deceiving yourself about who you are. Your self-deception might eventually run so deep that you are able to deceive those around you easily and without remorse.

Description

Your type has been called The Initiator, Succeeder, Performer, Achiever, and Motivator. You are decisive, risk-taking, adaptable, and optimistic. Your energy and motivation are usually much greater than the others. You expect success from yourself, and you usually get it.

You are good at juggling multiple commitments at a time and you rarely relax. Even when you are enjoying hobbies or spending time with friends, you are usually looking for recognition for being successful. You feel you may not have value outside of your achievements. You fear failure because your image and self-worth are wrapped up in what you *do* and not who you *are*.

Some of your best qualities are your ability to take initiative and get things done. You are adaptable and good at figuring out what others expect of you, and then meeting those expectations. At your best, you can achieve great things and inspire greatness in others.

Underneath your image of achievement is a tendency to brush aside your feelings and pretend everything is fine, even if you are suffering from extreme anxiety or depression. You feel enormous pressure to be outstanding, and you fear to stop to rest might lead you to failure.

As a member of the *Feeling Triad*, you struggle with shame. Your shame is centered around any inner qualities that you think are inadequate, and you deal with it by identifying with people that you see as successful.

Wings

The personalities to either side of you on the Enneagram are Two, the Helper, and Four, the Individualist. A Three with a Two-Wing has been labeled "The Charmer" by some, and a Three with a Four-Wing has been labeled "The Professional." Read the chapters on these two personalities to decide if you identify more strongly with one of them.

Directions of Integration and Disintegration

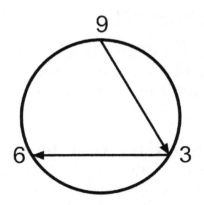

Your integration is toward type Six, the Loyalist. This means that when you are emotionally healthy, you exhibit qualities of a healthy Six. When you let go of your fears of failure, you are less competitive and cooperate with others. You find value from sharing goals and offering support. You may learn to ask for help for yourself and to trust others. In this reliance on others, you can become more selfless and act like a leader.

If you are less emotionally healthy but still secure, you display traits of average Sixes. When you are feeling sure of yourself, you can admit your anxieties to a few trusted people. For example, you may be able to maintain your image of achievement all day at the office, but you come home in the evening and unload your issues to a sympathetic partner.

Your disintegration is towards Nine, the Peacemaker. When you are under too much pressure for too long, you may start to just "go through the motions" to get through the day. You still maintain the appearance of accomplishing things for a while, but as stress continues, you might just shut down and withdraw from people.

Levels of Development

The following is a very brief breakdown of your levels of development as a Two, so you can begin to recognize your psychological health and warning signs of deterioration.

- **Healthy**
  - **Level 1 (at your best):** You let go of dependency on applause and believe in your intrinsic value. Working cooperatively with others is your authentic self.

84

- o **Level 2:** You are self-assured and energetic. Others are drawn to your charm and grace.
- o **Level 3:** You strive to be your best and inspire others.

- **Average**
  - o **Level 4:** You are driven to be the best. You worry about performing well and fear failure. You compare yourself to others.
  - o **Level 5:** You worry about how others see you; you hide your inner qualities under attributes you believe will make you look successful.
  - o **Level 6**: You feel jealous of others and their success, but on the outside, you appear arrogant. You try to impress others.

- **Unhealthy**
  - o **Level 7:** You fear humiliation and are willing to be unethical to maintain your image of success.
  - o **Level 8:** You are immoral in your attempts to hide your mistakes. You are very jealous of others and willing to hurt them in order to win.
  - o **Level 9:** You lose touch with reality and attempt to sabotage others. You obsessively hide or destroy any evidence of failures. Possible Narcissistic Personality Disorder.

Subtypes/Instincts

If you are a *social* Three, you seek tangible recognition so others may see your achievements. You adapt into any environment so you can avoid humiliation and be accepted everywhere. Because you are such a chameleon, you may lose track of your goals and become less of an achiever. You may be distracted by the need to impress your peers and stop pursuing tangible successes.

If you are a *sexual* Three, you aim to be as desirable as possible. Potential mates may see you as very charming and attractive, but your insecurities might keep you from being intimate with anyone. You wish to be appreciated for your inner qualities, but you fear to reveal these qualities because others may reject you.

Finally, as a *self-preservation* Three, you may be a "workaholic." You find worth in your ability to provide for yourself or your family. You are so driven by this priority that you cannot slow down or take time off. This addiction to work affects personal relationships and your physical health. Your family and/or significant others may not understand that you show love by working hard to provide for them.

Psychological and Spiritual Growth

As a Three, you can grow by realizing that your feelings and inner qualities do not have to be separate from your success and value. If you can get in touch with your emotions, you will find that you are able to function better as a whole human being. Thus, you find satisfaction in your work and relationships instead of wrapping your self-worth up in achievement.

Try slowing your pace and notice what happens to you internally and externally. Welcome feelings as normal parts of being human. Try to listen to someone without agenda. Instead of obeying the urge to self-promote or look good, tune in to what someone else is saying and try not to interrupt.

Your fear of failure cripples your intrinsic self-worth, so you pay more attention to people who are "winners." Try finding value in all people and realizing that they are much more than the image that they present to the public. Then, try that strategy on yourself. Exercise compassion and self-forgiveness when you feel you have failed and remember that making mistakes is part of being human. Failures are opportunities for growth.

Finally, remind yourself that everything is not dependent on your efforts. When you stop racing around to pursue achievement, you are present in the moment and there for your loved ones. Speaking of loved ones, remind yourself that they value you for who you *are*, not for what you *do!*

One Three shared that, after learning from the Enneagram, she learned to seek less approval from the outside world and stop finding worth in achievement. Before, she had believed in the core that she needed to be seen as successful. She would take any unsettling emotions and use them to fuel some sort of productivity, but this would cut off her ability to be in touch with those emotions. She felt like people would abandon her if she made a mistake.

Now that she has worked on herself through Enneagram teachings and therapy, this Three says that she needs less approval from others. She can admit when she makes a mistake without trying to cover up the truth. She can be honest with herself about her inner emotions and deal with them more effectively as they come up.

She says that she now feels like she is able to work more cooperatively with people and she is able to prioritize people over accomplishments. Her relationships have more meaning now, and she is able to make true friends more than she could before.

If you feel that your sense of acceptance and approval come from your achievements and you are terrified of failure, you're not alone! You can find help and healing by becoming vulnerable and recognizing your emotions, no matter how unsettling they are.

Relationships

This final section consists of lists with helpful hints *for* Threes in relationships and for people in relationships *with* Threes. These include business relationships, romantic relationships, and parent-child relationships.

Business Relationships FOR *Threes:*
- Work on developing patience for others who do not work as quickly as you.
- Slow your pace and devote yourself to the process.
- Admit mistakes and find opportunities for growth from them.
- Work with others instead of competing.
- Find ways to make your everyday duties creative.
- Listen to others when in a meeting and take a back seat.

Business Relationships WITH *Threes:*
- Let them know you appreciate their work.
- Speed up in talking to them.
- Avoid getting in the way of their progress or taking too much of their time.
- Join them in being active and getting results.
- When conflicts arise, let them vent if they are staying on task.

- Remind them people are more important than achievement.
- Remind them success can come from many different styles.
- Give honest but not overly judgmental feedback.

Parenting FOR *Threes:*
- You are good at being consistent, dependable, and loyal. Keep it up!
- Don't cut your time with your children short so that you can work more.
- It's ok to expect your children to be responsible but don't be too rigid.
- Don't punish them harshly for mistakes.
- Allow them to explore different activities without expecting a particular result.

Parenting When Your CHILD *Is A Three*
- Tell them you are proud of their accomplishments.
- Show appreciation for traits that have nothing to do with accomplishment—like generosity, honesty, and fairness.
- Foster an environment of peace and harmony at home.
- Tell them you enjoy being around them.
- Encourage them to try new things that do not have to become a competition.
- Model expressing feelings, doubts, and admitting mistakes at home.

Romantic Relationships FOR *Threes:*
- Remind yourself that your partner loves you for who you *are*, not what you *do*.
- Learn to develop empathy and understanding for yourself and your significant other.

- Practice telling them when experiencing doubts or anxieties.
- Be truthful about real feelings.
- Genuinely listen to them, without letting your mind race about what you should be accomplishing.
- Enjoy simple activities together, like taking walks.
- Let them decide what you do together sometimes.

Romantic Relationships WITH *Threes:*
- Treat them with love and compassion when they feel that they have failed.
- Encourage them to take time to "smell the roses," pay attention to feelings, and really listen to you.
- Show and tell them what is important to you.
- Tell them that you like being around them.
- Tell them when you're proud of them or their accomplishments.
- Give them honest feedback, without being overly judgmental.
- Encourage them to slow down and pay attention to their well-being.
- Tell them you value them for who they are.

Chapter 9: Type 4 – The Individualist

Type 4 Checklist: *Ask yourself if the following statements are true for you.*

- You are in touch with your emotions and listen to what they are telling you.
- At times, you are deeply in touch with human nature.
- You like to creatively express yourself.
- You can become quite self-absorbed.
- You are comfortable telling others how you feel.
- You thrive on being an individual, but sometimes, you wish you weren't so different from others.
- You care about beauty and personal taste.
- You feel alone and misunderstood.
- People have accused you of being over-dramatic and too sensitive.
- You find ways to be unique, no matter what you are doing.
- Sometimes, you feel very empty and depressed.
- You feel that there is something out there that would make you feel more whole and complete.
- You tend to compare yourself to others and are envious when you feel they have something you are missing in life.
- You have trouble planning things in advance.
- You admire what is beautiful, truthful, and noble in life.

If you can relate to more than half of the above statements, you are likely a Four or have a strong Four wing. Keep reading to learn more about your type!

Core Belief

The belief driving your behavior is that something important is missing in your life, and you must find it. You feel that your purpose is to express your authentic self and create beauty and meaning in life.

Avoidance: *Being Ordinary*

You fear and avoid what you view as common and insignificant in life because you feel these things have no worth. Deep down, you are afraid that you are missing the things that would make you truly unique, so you conceal what you think is ordinary.

Trap: *Being Unique*

You can be so ensnared by your goal of being different that you continually focus on what is missing in your life. As a result, you are unable to see and appreciate who you really are or what is good in your world.
Idealization: *I am authentic.*

You strive to distinguish yourself from others by emphasizing everything that is different about you. You find your value in this self-image.

Defense Mechanism: *Introjection*

Through introjection, you pick up traits that you view as unique and special to set yourself apart. This helps you avoid and overcome the ordinariness that you fear. You also internalize blame when things go wrong. This reinforces your feelings of loneliness and being misunderstood.

Passion: *Envy*

You incessantly compare yourself to others, both consciously and unconsciously. You feel something is missing from your life and you envy those who seem to have this "something." You feel you are somehow unlucky or that you have suffered more than others, and you have trouble feeling good about yourself.

Description

You maintain your identity by seeing yourself as different from others on a fundamental level. Your sense of individuality comes from being unique and special, but also from feeling that something important is missing from your life.

Some of your strengths are your abilities to experience feelings on a deep level and find meaning in life. You are very expressive, and you often can describe feelings and experiences in a very eloquent way. Your emotional honesty inspires others to get in touch with their own inner experiences and emotions. You can be very empathetic, supportive, passionate, and witty. You easily form bonds with other people, and you can be an excellent listener.

At times, you become completely preoccupied with your emotions and drift away into your thoughts and memories. You need to be different makes you feel alone and misunderstood. You feel that "something" is missing, although you may not be able to define what that

93

"something" is. You long for someone to come into your life and appreciate you for all your uniqueness.

You often suffer from low self-esteem. As a member of the *Feeling Triad*, you struggle with shame centered around your identity. You avoid this shame by focusing on your uniqueness.

You might have created a fantasy self – an imagined self-image with the individuality and special qualities you think you are missing. You try to project the image of this fantasy self, but you feel depressed about who you really are. Sometimes you imagine that others have much worse opinions of you than they do, and you can become extremely sensitive to how they treat you. You hold on to resentments towards people who have hurt you in the past.

Directions of Integration and Disintegration

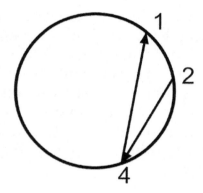

Your integration is towards type One, the Reformer. When you are emotionally healthy, you look like a healthy One. You start to notice how preoccupied you have been with your "unique disadvantages" and realize this is unhealthy. You see yourself more realistically and gain acceptance of your true self. You become practical and grounded, and you have a desire to help with worthwhile pursuits to benefit others.

If you are less healthy but still secure, you display the traits of average Ones, becoming more impatient and critical of other people than you usually are. Instead of silently comparing yourself to others, you begin to focus on their faults and become irritable. You may want to stay constantly busy and work towards improvement without stopping.

Your disintegration is towards type Two, the Helper. When emotionally wounded, you first withdraw from people. Once you realize that you are probably driving people away, you try "people pleasing" for a while, trying to make people need you by being constantly helpful. If this phase of discontent and emotional manipulation lasts, you become clingy and possessive of your loved ones.

Levels of Development

The following is a very brief breakdown of your levels of development as a Two, so you can begin to recognize your psychological health and warning signs of emotional deterioration.

- **Healthy**
    - o **Level 1 (at your best):** You let go of your belief that you are missing something and your projected uniqueness. Your creativity is inspirational to others.
    - o **Level 2:** You strive to have a meaningful identity based on your inner, true self. You

are aware of your feelings and intuitive to others.
  - **Level 3:** You are emotionally honest and strong, can express vulnerability, and remain true to yourself. You relate to others authentically.

- **Average**
  - **Level 4:** You work prolong emotions and promote an image of "the special one." You are dramatic and can withdraw into imagination.
  - **Level 5:** You manipulate others into treating you with special care. You struggle with envy if people around you are happy.
  - **Level 6**: You feel sorry for yourself and treating others as if they have no value. You believe you don't need to conform to the rules that apply to everyone else. You escape into a fantasy world.

- **Unhealthy**
  - **Level 7:** You resent life because of all the disappointments you have suffered. You reject anyone that does not support your emotional demands. You loathe yourself and are too fatigued to function.
  - **Level 8:** You hate yourself to the point of delusion and feel tormented by life. You blame yourself and everyone else, and you refuse to accept help.
  - **Level 9:** You reach despair and self-destruction. You may abuse addictive substances and are at risk of suicidal tendencies. Possible Avoidant, Depressive, or Narcissistic personality disorders.

Subtypes/Instincts

If you are a *social* Four, you want desperately to belong to a social crowd but fear that you don't fit in. You create a false image that is less restrained than you feel; even though you know this is a lie, you use it to feel like you belong. You express your individuality through your own personal style, but you are also trying to hide your insecurities and shame. When stressed, you withdraw from social contact almost completely for a time.

If you are a *sexual* Four, you have the potential for great intimacy in relationships. You may become quickly infatuated or possessive of a significant other. You believe you will feel complete by finding that "missing something" in the right person and place high expectations on your romantic partners. When these expectations are unmet, you become resentful, switching from feeling love to hate at a moment's notice. Your emotional nature can be both attractive and off-putting to others.

Finally, as a *self-preservation* Four, you look for fulfillment in luxury and comfort. Your envy fuels your need for expensive things, and you may indulge yourself in special luxuries when you are dealing with emotional pain. This may go to the extreme of addictive substances or behaviors when you feel your environment is not meeting your emotional needs.

Recommendations for Psychological and Spiritual Growth

As a Four, you grow by learning to move beyond the pain of your past and appreciating and accepting the present moment. Though you have been hurt or disappointed, you are not lacking anything as a human being. If you begin practice focusing on gratitude for what you have instead of mourning what you feel is missing, you find satisfaction and accept that wholeness exists right now, in the present moment.

Your value comes from being yourself, not from setting yourself apart. Try appreciating the "ordinary" traits in yourself and in others. You may even benefit from writing down commonplace things and characteristics that you appreciate as you go about your daily life.

You often experience very intense emotions that can be confusing or even debilitating. Remind yourself that feelings aren't facts, and feelings change all the time. Maintain a steady course of action even when you are experiencing intense feelings. Acknowledge and accept your feelings while refusing to be dominated by them.

You have been expecting others to focus on you. When you find yourself monopolizing conversational focus, gently redirect the attention back to other people. You may have to do this often, but it will get easier with practice. Build up others in your conversations and see how much joy you feel by making them happy. By cultivating happiness in others, you can start to overcome your envy and longing for that mysterious "something" that is missing.

One particular type Four says he is now discovering how to deal with his reckless behavior tendencies after learning from the Enneagram. He says that he often engages in risky behavior after enough emotional pressure has built up inside him. He behaves recklessly because he feels that he has to do something, anything, to break free from the feeling of pressure inside.

After studying the Enneagram, this Four is now more aware of the times when tension builds up inside him. Often, when he feels the urge to do something reckless, he talks to someone who is more rational than himself. If they are shocked at what he wants to do, he realizes that he is being irrational and that he needs to reflect on the emotions inside him that are making him feel that way. In this way, he is able to balance his extreme tendencies and he is becoming more in touch with himself.

Perhaps you, too, tend to act irrationally when you feel too much pressure inside you. Please understand that this tendency can be damaging to yourself and the people around you. You can unlearn this behavior by being willing to explore your feelings without letting them dominate you!

Relationships

This section consists of lists with helpful hints *for* Fours in relationships and for people in relationships *with* Fours. These include business relationships, romantic relationships, and parent-child relationships.

Business Relationships FOR *Fours:*
- You have been self-conscious in front of groups. Take on a role that will put you in front of people so you can practice and grow more comfortable.
- Stay connected with people by asking them about the details of their lives and complimenting their ideas.
- Plan to stay productive even when experiencing intense emotions.
- Appreciate the small, ordinary things that other people do at the workplace.

- When you feel criticized, pause instead of reacting. Try to learn and grow from this experience.
- Keep a list of your positive qualities in a place that you can access it easily when you are filled with self-doubt.

Business Relationships WITH *Fours:*
- Appreciate their emotional sensitivity and creativity.
- Avoid insisting they "calm down" or telling them they're overreacting.
- Join them in valuing individualism.
- In conflict, challenge them to stick to middle ground instead of withdrawing or having an angry outburst.
- Not taking what they say when they are angry or upset literary is advised since it might just be a temporary feeling.
- Encourage them to express their thoughts safely and directly instead of falling into a pit of depression.
- Compliment them when they do something well.

Parenting FOR *Fours:*
- You're good at supporting creativity and originality. Keep it up!
- You have a natural ability to get in touch with your feelings, so help your child learn how to do this too.
- Don't escape into your head or become too self-absorbed; remain present for your child.
- Don't be too critical.
- Watch your level of protectiveness. Some are good; too much can be damaging.

Parenting When Your CHILD *Is A Four*
- Be careful with criticism, as they are very sensitive.

- Encourage their imagination through artistic or other pursuits.
- Tell them you enjoy spending time with them.
- Encourage them to be grateful for ordinary things.
- Ask them to tell you about their feelings.
- Remind them that you love them just as they are and they don't need anything else to be worthy of your love.

Romantic Relationships FOR *Fours:*
- Focus on all the positive things about your partner and your relationship, even the small "ordinary" things.
- When you feel overwhelmed by emotions, don't unleash them all at once on your unsuspecting partner. Take deep breaths and try to explain it logically.
- Focus on your significant other in conversation at least as often as you focus on yourself.
- Remind yourself that your feelings aren't the only reality.
- Resist the urge to "punish" your partner when you feel neglected.
- Don't expect your partner to complete you. You are two individuals who enjoy each other's company and enhance each other's lives.

Romantic Relationships WITH *Fours:*
- Expect mood shifts that are unrelated to what you do or don't do.
- Try to remain steady, calm, and reliable under pressure.
- Set boundaries about your availability; don't succumb to attempts to monopolize your time.
- Give space in times of moodiness.

- Encourage them to slowly take in genuine compliments and bring these compliments to their attention if they don't notice them.
- Expect them to pursue you when you are distant and push you away when you are available.
- Don't tell them they are too sensitive or overreacting.
- Help them learn to love and value themselves.
- Appreciate their gifts of insight and empathy.
- Help them fight their inner critic and support them as they learn to express their feelings directly.

The Thinking Triad
(Types 5, 6, & 7)

Chapter 10: Type 5 – The Investigator

Type 5 Checklist: *Ask yourself if the following statements are true for you.*

- You can be highly innovative and inventive.
- You look beneath the surface of things to arrive at deep insights.
- You are independent and may be labeled as a "loner" or "misfit."
- You are happy to pursue your interests and curiosity wherever they take you.
- You have an exceptional ability to focus your attention.
- You can be so focused that you forget your surroundings or to take care of yourself.
- You enjoy spending time with people who have intelligence and interests you respect.
- You're full of knowledge, ideas, and opinions.
- You want to find someone to connect with but are afraid of losing your self-reliance.
- You fear you aren't equipped to face life, so you prefer to retreat into your mind.
- You're not comfortable dealing with your own emotions.

- You are shy, non-intrusive, independent, and reluctant to seek help.
- You're not usually comfortable with your social skills.
- When you make friends, you are devoted, and form lifelong attachments.
- You rarely or never experience boredom.

If you can relate to more than half of the above statements, you're probably a Five or you have a strong Five wing. Keep reading to learn more about your type!

Core Belief

The belief driving your behavior is that you must protect yourself from a world that gives too little and demands too much. Your unconscious fear is that there may not be enough resources for everyone to survive. You seek self-sufficiency and make few demands on others. You withdraw into your private world of thought to protect yourself from the world. By not making demands, you feel as if you are conserving resources and guaranteeing your own survival.

Avoidance: *Scarcity and Intrusion*

You fear and avoid intrusion of others who might make demands on your resources and energy. Your privacy, vast accumulation of knowledge and self-sufficiency protect you from expending too much of your energy. You fear you are not well-equipped for life, so you avoid intrusion of others so your inadequacy will not be exposed.

Trap: *Detaching to Study*

You enjoy escaping into your own mind and accumulating knowledge. You seek to build your confidence and ability to face the world through your intelligence. However, this habit can become so all-consuming that you neglect your emotional health and relationships.

Idealization: *I am wise and competent.*

You focus your energy on projecting the image that you are knowledgeable. You feel that knowledge is scarce and extremely valuable, so you equip yourself with as much of it as possible to survive.

Defense Mechanism: *Isolation*

Through isolation, you avoid feeling overwhelmed and empty. You retreat into your mind as a way of cutting yourself off from feelings. You may also isolate different parts of your life, such as keeping your work life entirely separate from your personal life. You may separate relationships so that your friends never meet each other. The purpose of all this isolation is to eliminate the risk of being exposed as inadequate and ill-equipped for life.

Passion: *Avarice (Hoarding)*

Although you appear intellectually competent, you lack confidence in yourself. You feel other people's demands might be too much for you and you won't be able to meet them. You "hoard" your time and energy by keeping as much of it to yourself as possible because you feel that you will not be enough to meet the needs of others.

Description

You value knowledge, understanding, and insight highly and you view your journey as one of constant learning. Your learning is mainly observational, and you seek to gain as much knowledge as possible about particular subjects.

Many, like you, have made significant discoveries and advances in various fields; at your best, you are brilliantly innovative! Your powers of observation, perception, and concentration are remarkable. Your active mind keeps you from ever being bored.

You take pride in being self-sufficient; by not depending on anyone or having anyone depend on you, you feel you are conserving what little resources you might have for making it through this life. As a member of the *Thinking Triad*, you deal with anxiety. Your anxiety is about your ability to face the outside world, and you cope with it by withdrawing and attempting to gain enough knowledge to become competent.

Although you isolate, you still sometimes crave the company of others. You make excellent company for those who are interested in your knowledge. Others find you a bit odd but interesting. Sometimes, you resemble the image of the "absent-minded professor" who is so caught up in his own studies and thoughts that he forgets to feed himself, is late for meetings, and doesn't hear the phone ring.

Directions of Integration and Disintegration

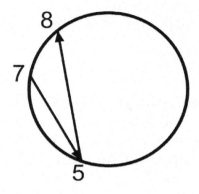

Your direction of integration is Eight, the Challenger. When you are emotionally healthy, you resemble a healthy Eight. When you see that your isolation is harmful to your psychological health, you try making more contact with yourself and others. As you become more in tune with yourself and reality, you will display the qualities of a good leader (a healthy Eight). You find you can help others with your expertise.

If you are less healthy but still secure, you look like an average Eight. When you are feeling sure of yourself, you assert your boundaries more aggressively, possibly becoming confrontational and controlling.

Your direction of disintegration is type Seven, the Enthusiast. You react to stress by isolating, but eventually, you start to need some interaction with others. Nervous energy builds up in you so that you become restless and anxious. Your behavior becomes erratic and impulsive, and you may become very talkative.

Levels of Development

The following is a very brief breakdown of your levels of development as a Five, so you can begin to recognize your psychological health and warning signs of emotional deterioration:

- **Healthy**
  - o **Level 1 (at your best):** Your self-image is not attached to your knowledge. You are wise, connected to your environment, and participate in life. You become a visionary and make exciting new discoveries.
  - o **Level 2:** You are fascinated by observing life. You notice everything, concentrate fully, and remain mentally alert.
  - o **Level 3:** You are an expert field. You are very independent and somewhat quirky.

- **Average**
  - o **Level 4:** You study and think extensively before acting. You are very intellectual and specialized in your knowledge.
  - o **Level 5:** You spend a lot of time escaping into your thoughts and detaching from reality. Your strongest interests may be strange or disturbing.
  - o **Level 6**: You resent anyone and anything that intrudes on your isolation and study time. You are purposefully argumentative and antagonistic.

- **Unhealthy**
  - o **Level 7:** You grow radically isolated and eccentric. You are emotionally unstable and antisocial.

- o **Level 8:** You become obsessed with disturbing ideas which fascinate and disturb you at the same time. At this point, you are delusional.
- o **Level 9:** You are so out of touch with reality that you may become self-destructive and deranged. Possibly Schizoid Avoidant or Schizotypal personality disorder.

Subtypes/Instincts

If you are a *social* Five, you are more outgoing than most other Fives. Your comfort in social situations depends on having some area of expertise to talk about or some skill to demonstrate. You may look down on those around you, feeling that they might not be able to understand your superior intelligence.

As a *sexual* Five, you desire intimacy and connection than most other Fives. This conflicts with your impulse to withdraw and isolate, so you are cautious and selective about who you get close to. You believe others will find you odd or even disturbing. Your desire is to find someone to share your private world of knowledge while helping you survive the life for which you feel ill-equipped.

Finally, if you are a *self-preservation* Five, you can be the most isolated. You are extremely private and withdrawn, but you do not focus on accumulating physical comforts. You spend a great amount of time alone, but you may socialize with a few people that you trust. If you do not live alone, you need some special place that is your own, where no one can intrude upon your solace.

Psychological and Spiritual Growth

Your growth as a Five takes place when you start putting yourself in the world. You believed you would gain confidence from studying, but it comes from experience. If you practice being present in your physical body and emotions instead of retreating to your mind, you will become more grounded and balanced. You have been denying that you even have emotions, but you feel things deeply. You need to learn how to experience those emotions at the moment and express them as they come.

When you feel the urge to withdraw and isolate, try to stay connected for just a little longer before retreating. Gradually allow more people into the circle of those you trust and practice talking about personal matters to those people. When you are with acquaintances outside of your circle of friends, try sharing something you wouldn't normally share. Pay attention to how long you talk – you may tend to talk too little or too long. Watch your audience for cues to see if you should talk more or less. Are they bored? Interested? Wanting to hear more? It may help to observe the interactions between other people to pick up on conversational skills.

There is more to you than your mind. Get in touch with your body by taking up some kind of physical activity. This could be anything from intense exercise to cooking or knitting. Try engaging in physical activities with friends or family.

You have been conserving your time and energy for fear of not having enough to go around, but you can now try to share with others. If you see an opportunity to be of service and want to help, give it a try. You may find that you feel more connected to the human race and more fulfilled as a result.

Because you have suppressed parts of yourself for so long, you may even want to seek expert help with getting in touch with your emotional and physical self. In the chapter about Type Nine, the Peacemaker, we mentioned bioenergetic work, which can also be helpful for Fives.

In describing his experience of learning from the Enneagram, one Five proclaims that bioenergetic work truly helped him to get in touch with his emotions. His instructor kept up a conversation with him while he engaged in the physical work of the session. When this Five experienced intense emotion during the session, the instructor had him strike a pillow with a tennis racquet! This technique proved very effective, allowing him to release his control over his emotions and let them come out.

This Five explains that, after this session, he realized how much pent-up rage and fear he had never recognized within himself. Once he became aware of his hidden emotions, he said that they no longer had the power to control him.

If you are a Five who struggles with the concept of being in touch with your emotions, you can find help also. There are many possible ways for you to accomplish this, including bioenergetic work. The important thing is for you to realize that you can start to feel more whole by getting in touch with your emotions and staying grounded in the world instead of retreating from it.

Relationships

This final section consists of lists with helpful hints *for* Fives in relationships and for people in relationships *with* Fives. These include business relationships, romantic relationships, and parent-child relationships.

Business Relationships FOR *Fives:*
- Try sharing and giving more of yourself, while taking in more support from others.
- When you feel the need to talk endlessly on a subject, pause and wait to see if anyone expresses interest in that subject.
- Know if you are just using your knowledge just to impress people.
- Bring your mind to the present by having a watch that beeps hourly. Be productive and be aware always of the present.
- Pay attention to the contributions of others and let them know when they are appreciated.
- Try reaching out to someone at work that is struggling, even if this makes you uncomfortable at first.

Business Relationships WITH *Fives:*
- Approach them slowly and thoughtfully.
- Value knowledge and talk about ideas together.
- Give them time to think things over; don't pressure them to make decisions immediately.
- Ask them to directly communicate with you and don't just assume.
- When conflicts arise, agree to disagree if possible.
- Challenge them to stay present when they want to withdraw.
- Give them a lot of information.

Parenting FOR *Fives:*
- You are likely good, very perceptive, kind, and devoted to your child. Keep it up!
- Avoid being over-demanding. Set fair expectations and communicate with them clearly.
- Research what is developmentally appropriate for your child's intellectual progress; do not expect too much from them.
- Allow your child to express strong emotions. Ask them to explain how they feel and why, if they are able.
- If your child is not a Five, you can still encourage them to read and learn about subjects that interest them.

Parenting When Your CHILD *Is A Five*
- They may spend a lot of time alone reading or making collections; take an interest in these hobbies with them.
- Let them know when you are proud of their achievements.
- Encourage them to get involved in events rather than just observing.
- When they look calm, they may be hiding anxiety. Don't assume they are fine just because they are not expressing emotions.
- Respect their need for alone time but set expectations for how much time they spend interacting with you and the family.
- They are sensitive and avoid conflict. Ask them regularly how they feel about different situations and people.

Romantic Relationships FOR *Fives:*
- Practice revealing personal matters and feelings to your partner. Ask them for patience and sympathy as you learn this new skill.
- If you feel the urge to withdraw because your partner is expressing emotions, stand your ground and practice deep breathing while remaining present and listening.
- Include the setting of limits and ask for what you want.
- Let them know what you value about them.
- Share equal time with them in conversation instead of monopolizing the time by talking about your areas of expertise.
- Spend time in some kind of physical activity together.

Romantic Relationships WITH *Fives:*
- Giving and respecting their alone time is not a rejection.
- Assure them that they can safely share their personal experiences and feelings by giving them the time and space they need to do so.
- Don't pressure them for fast decisions or immediate contact.
- Let them communicate with you directly and don't make assumptions.
- Learn a little about their areas of expertise so you can participate in conversations about these.
- Be independent, not clingy.
- Speak in a straightforward manner.
- If they seem aloof or distant, they may be feeling uncomfortable.
- Support them in situations when they are extremely uncomfortable. For example, help them

to endure a short time at a big party and then gracefully take your leave together.

- Take time to vocally appreciate their gifts of observation, perception, and focus.

Chapter 11: Type 6 – The Loyalist

Type 6 Checklist: *Ask yourself if the following statements are true for you.*

- You are meticulous, disciplined, and persevering.
- You have a talent for seeing potential problems and dealing with them before they get out of hand.
- You enjoy being of service and want to contribute to the world.
- You are good at heading up projects because you can organize resources and prioritize tasks well.
- You struggle with doubt and anxiety, usually finding plenty to worry about.
- Sometimes, you test people by provoking them to see how they will react.
- You are slow and cautious to commit, but once you do commit, you are loyal to a fault.
- You do not trust people quickly.
- You often do not have much faith in yourself.
- You prefer having a predictable environment.
- You often feel like you are looking for something or someone to believe in.
- You may complain about stress, but you thrive on it.
- You can be very stable, self-reliant, and courageous.
- You fear to be without support and guidance.
- You are fiercely loyal to ideas, systems, and beliefs that have proven themselves to you.

If you can relate to more than half of the above statements, chances are that you are a Six or you have a strong Six wing. Keep reading to learn more about your type!

Core Belief

The central belief that drives your behavior is that the world is a dangerous and threatening place. You believe that you need to be prepared and loyal so that people can count on you. You feel that not everyone can be trusted, and you cannot let your guard down. At the same time, you believe that you should not show any fear.

Avoidance: *Uncertainty, Vulnerability, and Deviance (from Group Norms)*

You have many inner anxieties and you try to calm them by trying to make your world predictable and trouble-free, even though this is impossible. Once you have found a group to be loyal to, you avoid any appearance of disloyalty such as deviating from the group norms.

Trap: *Creating Safety and Security*

You compulsively try to create a feeling of security through meticulous planning, attempts to anticipate problems, and distrusting people until they have proven themselves to you. Once you have committed to something or someone, you remain committed to a fault because you feel secure in that commitment. To detach would disrupt the safety that you treasure.

Idealization: *I am loyal.*

You want the people in your trusted circle to know they can count on you to guard their safety no matter what, even though you feel deep anxiety within yourself. You cultivate this image by trying to constantly be prepared for any eventuality.

Defense Mechanism: *Projection*

Projection is a method of attributing things to others that you cannot accept about yourself. If you think negatively about a friend but cannot admit it, you may accuse someone else of thinking negatively about them. Your projection is so thorough that you often imagine it to be true.

Passion: *Anxiety*

As a member of the *Thinking Triad*, your central emotional issue is anxiety. Your struggle with anxiety is much more central than types Five and Seven. You are continually on the look-out for dangers or problems and are particularly talented at imagining worst-case scenarios. Even though you try to be prepared for any scenario, your anxiety may be so extreme that you are too fearful to truly be prepared.

Brief Description

Your type has been called The Guardian, The Devil's Advocate, The Skeptic, The Questioner, or The Loyalist. You may like to believe you are realistic, but others think you are pessimistic.

Although it takes you a while to trust a person or organization, you are extremely loyal to them once they have proven themselves. You are loyal to the extent that you might hang on to people, beliefs, and groups much longer than they deserve. You fear to let go of them because you feel that you will not have support or guidance without them.

You have been accused of "overthinking" life issues. You second-guess yourself regularly and have trouble trusting your own thinking and judgments. You may have tremendous difficulty making big decisions, but you do not want anyone else to make those decisions for you either.

Some of your strengths are your ability to plan, attention to detail, courage, and preparedness. You are devoted to your values and very team-oriented. These qualities make you a valued contributor in many work environments. When emotionally healthy, you trust your inner instincts and you have the potential to be a powerful influence for worthy causes.

One thing that sets your type apart from others is that you seem to be a bundle of contradicting traits. You are simultaneously weak and strong, courageous and fearful, doubter and believer, passive and aggressive, and so on. When it comes to your issues with fear or anxiety, your response may be to surrender to the self-doubt or to confront it head-on. This unpredictability can be especially confusing to people who are close to you.

Directions of Integration and Disintegration

Your direction of integration is towards type Nine, the Peacemaker. This means that when you are emotionally healthy, you take on some of the characteristics of a healthy Nine. If you learn to trust yourself, you can relax and accept life circumstances without anxiety. You find that you can support other people because you are not doubtful of your own security anymore. You find inner quiet when you stop second-guessing yourself.

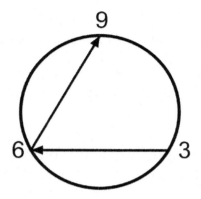

If you are less emotionally healthy but still, in secure conditions, you may display the traits of an average Nine, who deals with stress by shutting down and disengaging from life. In this state, you may prefer to numb yourself to life's stresses with comfortable routines.

Your direction of disintegration is toward type Three, the Achiever. Your first reaction to stress is to become extremely anxious but when stress is excessive, you leap into a mode of hyper-productivity. You try to deal with your anxieties and feelings of inadequacy by working hard and constantly getting things done. You may become so task-oriented that you damage relationships.

Levels of Development

The following is a very brief breakdown of your levels of development as a Six, so you can begin to recognize your psychological health and warning signs that you may have some work to do.

- **Healthy**
    - **Level 1 (at your best):** You find guidance within yourself and trust that you are secure. You are genuinely trustworthy and able to provide support and true emotional bonds.
    - **Level 2:** You are lovable and affectionate. You value trust and forming permanent relationships/alliances with others.
    - **Level 3:** You are responsible and reliable. You work hard to create security and stability in your world. You are dedicated to community causes that you believe in.

- **Average**
    - **Level 4:** You invest your energy in anything you think will bring you stability. You are constantly on the look-out for problems. You look outside yourself for safety.
    - **Level 5:** Your anxiety causes you to be reactive and pessimistic. You have trouble making decisions and are often too cautious to take any action. Your uncertainty makes you unpredictable.
    - **Level 6**: Your deep insecurities cause you to become defensive and blame others for your problems. You are controlling and suspicious, dealing with your fears by trying to instill them in others.

- **Unhealthy**
    - **Level 7:** You fear that your security is gone, so you begin to panic and seek safety elsewhere. Your feelings of inferiority cause you to belittle others and cause divisions.

- **Level 8:** You become paranoid that others are out to get you. You act irrationally and potentially violent.
- **Level 9:** You reach a level of hysteria and become self-destructive through suicidal ideations or addictive substances. Possible Passive-Aggressive or Paranoid personality disorders.

Subtypes/Instincts

If your dominant instinct is *social*, you look for security in your social connections. You make yourself valuable to a group by devoting your time and energy to it. By ingratiating yourself to a social circle, you hope to find the sense of security that you crave. You want others to see you as approachable and safe.

If you are a Six whose dominant instinct is *sexual*, you look for safety in your bond with a partner. You are emotionally intense because you are anxious about your ability to choose and keep the right mate, and because you have trouble trusting that your significant other will really be there for you. You feel the need to prove your desirability so that your mate will continue to find you attractive. Under stressful conditions, you may experience strong shifts in your feelings toward your partner.

Finally, if you are a Six who values *self-preservation* as your dominant instinct, you focus on protecting your physical resources, like money and food. You feel more secure when you are the one in charge of financial decisions, and you have trouble trusting other people to be responsible. You are more introverted than other Sixes. To protect your sense of security, you might stay in bad situations (like abusive relationships) longer than you should.

Psychological and Spiritual Growth

Your growth as a Six happens when you recognize that your security must come from within. There is no external relationship, structure, organization, or idea that will continually work to provide you with the sense of safety that you so desperately desire. You must learn to trust your instincts and ability to make decisions. This may take a lot of time and effort, but the reward of finding faith in yourself will be worth it.

You may think that you have more anxieties than most, but everyone experiences anxieties. When you are fearful, learn to recognize it and understand it instead of working frantically to alleviate it. Try learning a few calming breathing exercises.

Take a moment to think on your past anxieties and realize that few to none of your feared worst-case scenarios have ever come true. When you focus on the negative things that might happen, you only weaken yourself. Choose to strengthen yourself by focusing on the positive.

Try to trust people more freely and turn to them when you need help or a listening ear. You fear rejection, but it's important that you try to find someone trustworthy and allow yourself to get close to them. You have been desiring closer relationships but are fearful that people think badly of you. The truth is that most people probably think better of you than you realize.

One Six explains how she benefitted from Enneagram teachings and from learning how to do breathing exercises. Before, her fear of being hurt made her put up barriers. Rather than expressing any feelings, she kept other people out, telling herself that they couldn't be trusted. She was afraid of revealing much about herself because she thought people might use that information against her.

Because she wanted to experience a fuller life, she decided to learn of the Enneagram and breath work. Instead of being defensive all the time, she learned to soften her core. Breathing techniques helped her to sense her feelings and work out her aggression. She found that she could feel love along with other emotions and that she could let go of her suspicion towards others. She was relieved to discover that she was better able to relate to other people once she was more in touch with her inner self.

If you are a Six who has let your distrust of others keep you from them, there is hope for you. Breathing exercises can be one key to unlocking your inner self and finding the close relationships that you desire and deserve. Learn to trust and rely on others, and you will reap great rewards.

Relationships

This final section consists of lists with helpful hints *for* Sixes in relationships and for people in relationships *with* Sixes. These include business relationships, romantic relationships, and parent-child relationships.

Business Relationships FOR *Sixes:*
- Try balancing the negative spin you tend to put on situations with positives.

- Put your skills to good use by heading up projects, prioritizing tasks, and organizing details.
- Welcome tasks and situations that cause anxiety and move ahead into them. Focus on breathing through the fear.
- Instead of distrusting people until they prove themselves trustworthy, try trusting them until they prove themselves untrustworthy.
- Recognize your own concerns and emotions instead of projecting them on others.

Business Relationships WITH *Sixes:*
- Value their problem-solving skills; their attention to problems; come to an agreement on procedures and rules.
- Avoid changing the rules abruptly or withholding information.
- Try not to tell them their concerns are unfounded.
- Together, acknowledge the possibilities of things going wrong before you move ahead.
- When you sense conflict, don't be ambiguous. Show your cards as much as possible.
- Challenge them to take responsibility for their reactions instead of blaming external reasons.
- When possible, get them to see the humor in situations.

Parenting FOR *Sixes:*
- You are likely very loving and nurturing. Keep it up!
- You might be reluctant to give your child independence. Try to let go in stages, explaining your trust in them and your expectations a little at a time.
- Try not to be consumed with worry over your child's well-being. Do all you can to care for them and teach them to be safe, then let go of your

worry. You cannot control what happens to them every hour of the day, and bad things could happen with or without your worry.
- Work on setting boundaries and saying no when necessary. Your child will still love and respect you, and your secure bond will still be intact.

Parenting When Your CHILD *Is A Six*
- They may be over-anxious and hypervigilant. Try to help them alleviate their fears by talking about them.
- Assure them that they can trust you, but also train them to know what to do in case of emergency.
- Don't get in battles in which they might see you as the enemy. Instead, explain that your rules and expectations are there to protect them and help them grow into a confident and competent adult.
- Do your best to avoid unpredictability in the home. Provide a safe and nurturing environment in which they don't find excessive reasons for their anxiety.

Romantic Relationships FOR *Sixes:*
- Resist the urge to become suspicious and controlling. If you suddenly find that you want to question your partner's trustworthiness, ask yourself what emotions you are not addressing.
- Work on trusting them steadfastly unless and until they give you reasons to doubt them.
- Before you overreact, try to pause to reflect on what you are feeling and what prompted that emotion.
- Be aware of your pessimism, because it causes you to project negativity on your significant other.
- Learn to stay in the present moment with your partner.

- Discuss your insecurities instead of internalizing them and allowing them to change your attitudes and behavior.

Romantic Relationships WITH *Sixes:*
- Help them to face their fears directly.
- Carefully listen to them and be clear and direct.
- Anxiety doesn't define them, so don't judge them by just that.
- Reassure them that everything is ok between the two of you.
- Gently encourage them to try new experiences.
- When possible, try to lighten the mood by making jokes and laughing with them, not at them.
- Tell them you appreciate their commitment to you and others.
- Try spontaneous reassurances, romance, and occasional surprises.
- When they identify problem areas, don't argue with them. Recognize the issue. Even if you aren't ready to discuss it further, let them know you are committed to talking it through soon.
- Remind them that they are valuable to you.

Chapter 12: Type 7 – The Enthusiast

Type 7 Checklist: *Ask yourself if the following statements are true for you.*

- You are energetic and like to make a lot of plans.
- You don't see the point of denying yourself anything you enjoy.
- You are entrepreneurial and skilled at networking and self-promotion.
- If you focus your many talents and put your mind to something, you can be very successful.
- You have trouble focusing because you believe that something better might be waiting for you.
- You're afraid that everyone will find out that deep down, you feel empty inside.
- You like to keep your options open.
- You have a hard time empathizing with people in emotional pain.
- You are curious and adventurous.
- You tend to focus your energy on maintaining your freedom and happiness.
- You dislike feeling trapped or limited by having few options.
- You love to fill up your social calendar.
- You can be very creative.
- You bounce back quickly from setbacks and disappointments.
- You are often very slow to make commitments to people.

If you can relate to more than half of the above statements, you are probably a Seven or you have a strong Seven wing. Keep reading to learn more about your type!

Core Belief

The belief that drives your behavior is that the world limits and frustrates people and causes pain that you can escape by staying upbeat and keeping your possibilities open.

Avoidance: *Pain*

You flee from the emotional pain of the world by engaging in as many distractions and activities as possible.

Trap: *Imagining and Planning*

You can get so caught up in planning the next adventure or party that you never actually live in the moment or take the time to be aware of how you are feeling.

Idealization: *I am OK.*

You want everyone around you to believe that you are feeling great and having the time of your life, even though you may be hiding feelings of loneliness and emptiness. You may not even be aware of your inner pain.

Defense Mechanism: *Rationalization*

Through rationalization, you reframe negative experiences in a positive light. To help maintain the pretense of you being okay and prevent suffering, you are doing this reframing.

Passion: *Gluttony*

Because you constantly hide painful feelings that you aren't willing to acknowledge, you may seek constant stimulation to distract yourself. You greedily devour every experience you encounter. You never fully enjoy anything because you are always looking forward to the next thing.

Description

Your type has been called The Generalist, The Visionary, The Adventurer, The Epicure, or The Enthusiast. You constantly look at the bright side of everything, and your optimism draws other people to you. You are enthusiastic about almost everything that catches your attention, and you approach life with curiosity, optimism, and an adventurous spirit. You pursue what you want in life with cheerful determination.

Besides optimism, your strengths include a quick mind and the ability to pick up new information and skills quickly. These are great advantages but also make it difficult for you to decide what to do with yourself. Because learning comes easily to you, you may not appreciate your abilities as much as if you had to struggle to obtain them.

As a member of the *Thinking Triad*, your emotional issues center on anxiety, although this may not be as apparent as for Fives and Sixes. You are out of touch with your inner guidance; consequently, you doubt your ability to make decisions. You cope with this anxiety by keeping your mind excessively busy and by continually moving from one experience to the next.

At your core, you fear that you may not be able to find what you really want out of life. This fear prompts you to try everything, either to find what you want or to "settle" for a substitute and create a little enjoyment along the way. You live to fulfill your desire for freedom and variety.

Wings

The personalities to either side of you on the Enneagram are Six, the Loyalist, and Eight, the Challenger. A Seven with a Six-Wing has been labeled "The Entertainer" by some, and a Seven with an Eight-Wing has been labeled "The Realist." Read the chapters on Six and Eight to decide if you identify with one of these wings.

Directions of Integration and Disintegration

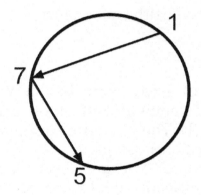

Your direction of integration is towards type Five, the Investigator. When you are emotionally healthy, you can resemble a healthy Five. If you learn to relax and tolerate uncomfortable feelings, you can focus more fully and use your gifts of creativity and insight. You become more productive by following your true interests.

If you are less emotionally healthy but still, in secure conditions, you may act like an average Five. When you get exhausted from all your adventurous Seven-ish tendencies, you might abruptly withdraw from your social life to rest and regroup.

Your direction of disintegration is towards type One, the Reformer. At times, you may feel frustrated that you are not accomplishing as much as you would like to because you have been jumping from one activity to another. When you feel this way, you act like an average One by trying to impose organization and control on yourself. This self-imposed order frustrates you more, and you become very critical with yourself and sometimes others.

Levels of Development

The following is a very brief breakdown of your levels of development as a Seven so you can begin to recognize your psychological health and warning signs of emotional deterioration.

- **Healthy**
  - **Level 1 (at your best):** You can live in each moment and enjoy each experience deeply. You have gratitude and appreciation for your blessings.
  - **Level 2:** You are cheerful, excitable, and enthusiastic about the experience. You very extroverted and spontaneous.
  - **Level 3:** You are multi-talented, productive, practical, and accomplished.

- **Average**
  - **Level 4:** You restlessly search for more options. You are adventurous but

unfocused, trying to keep up with the latest trends.

- o **Level 5:** You are hyperactive, self-indulgent, and uninhibited. You have many ideas but rarely follow through.
- o **Level 6**: Your over-consumption reaches addictive levels. You are greedy and selfish, insensitive, demanding, and unsatisfied.

- **Unhealthy**
    - o **Level 7:** You fall prey to addictions in an effort to quiet your anxieties. You are childish and impulsive.
    - o **Level 8:** Your moods change erratically and you act compulsively. You essentially are in flight from yourself.
    - o **Level 9:** You have ruined your health and used up your energy. You may become claustrophobic and panicky. Corresponds to depression, suicidal tendencies, possible Bipolar disorder, and Histrionic personality disorder.

Subtypes/Instincts

If you recall from Chapter 2, each person is equipped with three basic instincts – social, sexual, and self-preservation. As a Seven, one of these three is your dominant instinct, and it uniquely influences your personality traits.

If you are a *social* Seven, you are extremely people-oriented, so your adventure planning is focused on group activities. You like looking to worthy causes to invest your creative energies on because you feel like you have the power to effect positive change in the world. You don't like committing to any particular person or cause because that makes you feel trapped. This commitment-phobia sometimes hurts the feelings of your friends.

As a *sexual* Seven, you bring your curiosity and adventurous spirit to relationships. You love getting intensely involved with new people and your magnetic personality makes it easy for you to capture their attention. You frustrate yourself and others, though, because you can quickly shift focus to another person, idea, or thing that seems more exciting.

Finally, if you are a *self-preservation* Seven, you enjoy material possessions. You spend a lot of time planning to buy or experience various luxury items. You are good at hunting down a good bargain, and you seek friends who share your interests. Sometimes, you have unrealistic expectations and can end up disappointed because the material world cannot always meet your needs.

Psychological and Spiritual Growth Recommendations

Your growth as a Seven depends on you realizing that you can find happiness in the present by being still and recognizing beauty all around you. When you stop focusing on the future and looking for bigger and brighter adventures, you will be able to live in the moment and deeply enjoy each experience, no matter how ordinary it may seem. Being open to the enjoyment of the here and now can also bring awareness of the spiritual life beyond what you can see, taste, and feel.

Begin by recognizing your impulses and letting them pass instead of giving in to them. This helps you focus on things that will benefit you on a deeper level. If you find you still feel that you must act on an impulse, try putting it off for a day and see if you still have the same desire tomorrow.

Try to choose on quality over quantity in your experiences and relationships. This can be learned by giving your full attention to each experience and person that you become involved with. Focus your attention on them instead of rushing on to something newer and seemingly shinier. Ask yourself if what you desire is what will be good for you in the long run.

Work on really listening to people so that you can fully appreciate what they are communicating to you. Make and fulfill commitments and learn to become more aware of others' feelings.

As much as you try to avoid negative feelings and experiences, you need to try to realize that it is limiting and damaging to only seek the positive. By allowing pain and uncomfortable emotions, you are opening yourself to the full human experience. You will be rewarded for your openness with a much deeper satisfaction in your existence.

You may be inspired by the experience of a Seven who learned where she could find true joy. She used to avoid pain at all possible costs, but she discovered the Enneagram during a time of great unavoidable pain. She began learning about how she had spent her life fleeing from discomfort, and she gained the courage to stay grounded even while she was experiencing pain.

This Seven learned how to make more rational life choices, instead of blindly following impulses that arose when she was trying to avoid difficult feelings. She has discovered that she is able to sit and feel her emotions and let them pass through her, no matter how long it takes.

She now knows that when she suddenly feels intensely euphoric, she needs to be careful and slow down. She is learning to be present in each moment, no matter how ordinary it may seem. She has benefited immensely from tai chi and mindfulness practices. This enlightened Seven says that she sometimes misses the euphoric highs of being an unfettered Seven, but she has now found true joy and a sense of fulfillment in the here and now, thanks to her Enneagram work.

Take heart if you are a Seven who rushes from adventure to exhausting adventure in order to avoid feelings of pain and difficulty. You can also find lasting contentment in each moment as it passes if you take the time and do the work. You can learn to sit through your emotions, survive them and embrace them as a part of your true self.

Relationships

This final section consists of lists with helpful hints *for* Sevens in relationships and for people in relationships *with* Sevens. These include business relationships, romantic relationships, and parent-child relationships.

Business Relationships FOR *Sevens:*
- Work to focus on one task at a time.
- Fully listen to your coworkers and appreciate what they have to offer.
- Make an effort to stay the course with any idea or project you commit to.

- Try to adopt a realistic point of view. If something negative needs to be discussed, face it instead of avoiding it or reframing it.
- Calm your mind when you feel it racing ahead in a conversation or presentation.
- Use your optimism to the fullest by helping others see how they can learn from mistakes and setbacks.

Business Relationships WITH *Sevens:*
- Show appreciation for their stories and positive ideas.
- Don't be too negative. Also, don't insist to do a thing in just one way.
- Be with them while they're imagining new possibilities and having fun.
- When you sense conflict, challenge them to be responsible for the things they did wrong.
- Make them stop talking so that they can know what is needed from them by you or the other people.
- Encourage them in learning to calm their mind and be present in the moment.

Parenting FOR *Sevens:*
- You are good at helping children overcome challenges. Keep it up!
- Bring your creativity and sense of fun into your children's playtime. Help them foster their imagination.
- Try not to avoid the ordinary or negative so much that your children don't learn from their mistakes or grow up with unrealistic expectations from life.
- Don't over-commit. Only promise things that you can fulfill.
- Prioritize setting aside time for your children and don't violate that priority.

- Be mature in managing your disappointment if your family doesn't share your enthusiasm.
- Try to match your energy to that of your family.

Parenting When Your CHILD *Is A Seven*
- They are probably active and adventurous. Encourage these traits, but set boundaries.
- Help them rein in their excitement when it is inappropriate for a situation or place.
- Help them find activities where they can be around their peers.
- Encourage their imagination, but help them learn about focus and commitment by achieving one thing at a time and seeing projects through from beginning to end.
- Help them to appreciate the little things and point out the beauty of the ordinary things all around them.
- Applaud their optimism, but help them learn to express sadness and fear so they become comfortable with these feelings.

Romantic Relationships FOR *Sevens:*
- Learn to be present at the moment with your mate.
- Practice fully listening to what they have to say.
- When you feel boxed in and tempted to look for a shiny, new relationship, pause to remember all the wonderful things about who you are with now.
- When you feel hurt or confused, acknowledge it and don't try to reframe it in a positive light. Talk about it if you can.
- Appreciate the joy and beauty in day-to-day life with your significant other.
- Try to take any criticism as constructive, if it is intended in that way. Ask for clarification if necessary.

Romantic Relationships WITH *Sevens:*

- Know that you might feel either adored or ignored from moment to moment. Express why you are feeling that way.
- Be kind and gentle with any criticism. State the good news before the bad.
- Know that they are out of touch with negative emotions, and help them practice expressing them.
- Join them in enjoying creativity and planning fun adventures.
- Help them commit to projects or plans and see them through to the end.
- When they express boredom, know that they may be masking other feelings that are uncomfortable. Help them get in touch with these.
- Use kindness and thoughtfulness to help them express avoided emotions.
- Help them focus on realistic plans and staying in (and appreciating) the present.

Conclusion

Thank you for making it through to the end of *Enneagram Made Easy*. Let's hope it was informative and able to provide you with all of the tools you need to achieve your goals, whatever they may be.

The next step is to keep learning and growing! On the next page, we have included a helpful list of websites that are literal fonts of information on Enneagram-based learning and growth. Through these, you can delve further into any Enneagram-related topics that you wish to pursue. You'll find more tests to confirm your basic personality type. You will discover a dearth of information about various Enneagram types in relationships and in the business world. You will read about other enthusiasts' personal experiences of growth and self-discovery. You will find more suggestions for growth, meditations, and physical exercises that will benefit your personality type. You can find others seeking to learn more and find out where workshops and classes near you may be hosted. In online forums, you can find others of your type and begin communicating with each other. Our hope is that this book is just the beginning of your Enneagram journey to wholeness and spiritual health.

Finally, if you found this book useful in any way, a review on Amazon is always appreciated!

One last thing before you go – Can I ask a small favor? I need your help! If this book has been helpful to you, could you share your experience on Amazon by providing an honest feedback and review? This wouldn't take much of your time (a sentence will be very much appreciated), but a massive help for me and absolutely good Karma. Due to not having the backing of a big publication I don't have the big reach or promotion to get my books out to a bigger audience and rely heavily on my readers help, <u>I take out time to read every review and I'm usually extremely excited for every honest feedback I get. If my book was able to inspire you, please express it!</u> This will help position me at the top for others seeking for new ideas and reasonable knowledge to access easily.

I'm very grateful and I wish you every good things of life on your journey!

Warm regards,
Michael.

My Free Gift to You – <u>Get One of My Audiobooks For Free!</u>

If you've never created an account on Audible (the biggest audiobook store in the world), **you can claim one free** audiobook **of mine!**
It's a simple process:

1. Pick one of audiobooks on Audible: https://www.audible.com/search?keywords=michael+wilkinson&ref=a_search_t1_header_search

2. Once you choose a book and open its detail page click the orange button "Free with 30-Day Trial Membership."

3. Follow the instructions to create your account and download you first free audiobook.

Not that you are NOT obligated to continue after your free trial expires. You can cancel you free trial easily anytime and won't be charged at all.

About The Author

Hello,

My name is Michael. My life has been one amazing and a passionate journey, which I feel want everyone to be a part of or experience in one way or the other. I'm someone who believes there is more to life than what we already know. I endeavored many things to transform my life way more than my expectations to a very fulfilling one, and it's time I shared with you this interesting journey in order for you to apply it, as well.

I was a shy and quiet kid and had the typical young life, growing up in England doing the normal kids things, playing football, video games and didn't know much of what I wanted in life except that I loved cartoons. That was until I turned 18 and started to explore the world. That changed the way I saw things and everything in life, it opened my eyes to what was possible. I became very eager to learn new things and explore more.

My interests include traveling, practicing martial arts, self-development, and offering value by assisting other people. I've got a keen passion for contents relating to sociology, mediation, social psychology, eastern philosophy, communication skills, emotional intelligence, NLP, time management, mindfulness, and relevant studies related to self-development and being the best version of whom you are.

Calm down, smile, and express the life inside of you... I look forward to hearing from you soon!

Helpful Resources

https://www.enneagraminstitute.com

- Official website of The Enneagram Institute.
- In-depth information about each of the 9 types.
- Purchase a longer test to confirm your type.
- Learn more about relationships between different types.
- Find out about Enneagram workshops and other training.

https://www.enneagramworldwide.com

- Offers a structured curriculum for your personal development.
- Exploration through listening to personal experiences of others.
- Comparisons between Enneagram types.
- Description of instinctual subtypes.
- Further insight into applying the Enneagram to your life.

https://www.integrative9.com

- Uses the Enneagram to provide development solutions for individuals, teams, and organizations.
- Information and products about each of the 9 types as well as the subtypes.
- Specializes in products for organizations and teams.
- Worldwide training and events.

https://theenneagramatwork.com

- Features products and workshops geared toward individuals, businesses, and organizations.
- Information about Enneagram coaching and typing.
- In-depth articles on various Enneagram topics.
- Information about Enneagram types in the workplace, on teams, and as leaders.

https://www.9types.com

- Diagrams that illustrate the key motivations and behaviors of each type.
- In-depth looks at each type through the lenses of several important sources.
- Information on all possible combinations of romantic relationships between Enneagram types.

http://drdaviddaniels.com/the-enneagram/

- Recent and relevant Enneagram Blog topics.
- Registration for weekly reflections.
- Links to podcasts and videos.
- In-depth information about relationships for each type.
- Growth recommendations for each type.

http://www.enneagram-monthly.com

- A journal dedicated to Enneagram discussion and education.
- Narratives by and about each type.
- Link for subscribing to the full journal.

http://theenneagraminbusiness.com

- E-learning, resources and professional services geared towards learning about Enneagram types in organizations.
- Access consulting tools, training, coaching and retreats.
- Useful information about each Enneagram type in various roles of the business world.
- Certification programs, DVDs, etc. available in the store.

Bibliography

Cloete, Dirk. "Explore the 9 Enneagram Type Descriptions." Integrative 9: Enneagram Solutions, 2018, www.integrative9.com/enneagram/introduction/.

"Enneagram Types." The Narrative Enneagram, 2018, www.enneagramworldwide.com/tour-the-nine-types/.

O'Hanrahan, Peter. "Personal Stories." THE ENNEAGRAM AT WORK, 2018, theenneagramatwork.com/personal-stories/.

O'Hanrahan, Peter. "The Nine Enneagram Types." THE ENNEAGRAM AT WORK, 2018, theenneagramatwork.com/nine-enneagram-types/.

Riso, Don Richard., and Russ Hudson. Discovering Your Personality Type: the Essential Introduction to the Enneagram. Houghton Mifflin, 2003.

"The Nine Enneagram Type Descriptions." The Enneagram Institute, 2017, www.enneagraminstitute.com/type-descriptions/.

"Type Descriptions." 9types.Com, www.9types.com/descr/.

"Types." Enneagram Monthly, 2017, www.enneagram-monthly.com/types.html.

All images created by Rob Fitzel and used with permission from http://www.fitzel.ca/enneagram/graphics.html.

Made in the USA
Middletown, DE
28 November 2019